The

$100

Million

Dollar

Playbook

The

$100
Million
Dollar
Playbook

David Alan

Oakhill Press

10 9 8 7 6 5 4 3 2 1
Book production by Bookwrights Design
Cover design by Michael Kormarck
Edited by David Alan, Ed Helvey, & Mary Ellen Brice-Alan
Graphic Manipulation by David Alan & Ron Oostdyk
Printed in the United States of America

Library of Congress Cataloging-in-Publication Data
on file with the Publisher

ISBN 1-886939-54-3

Oakhill Press
1647 Cedar Grove Rd.
Winchester, VA 22603
800-32-BOOKS

DEDICATION

This book is dedicated to my wife, partner and best friend, Mary Ellen Brice-Alan, my mom, Edith S. Levin, and my son, Thomas Michael Brice.

CONTENTS

FOREWORD

When David asked me to do the foreword to his new book, needless to say, I was humbled and flattered.

David's wisdom and common sense is a refreshing experience. Only another author can know what it took to bring you this treasure. I say it's a treasure because of the great fortune it can bring you. This is much more than a moneymaking business book, it's a life improvement course, a course that I recommend you taking as a journey. George Bernard Shaw said, "The average person thinks only three times in their life." For many I think this is an exaggeration. I promise, you will exceed this in every chapter in *The $100 Million Dollar Playbook*.

David's grasp on the underlying motivations in advertising and sales is extraordinary. This book not only gives you the why, but the 'how to' in promoting your business and your life. He brings to the table a no nonsense approach with a psychological understanding from inside the consumer's shoes of what motivates people and why. This can benefit you immensely by giving you a better understanding of human nature and what motivates people to buy your goods, products or services.

I love David's new, unique concepts such as: Being a Dolphin, the Do Besters vs. the At Leasters, Y.C.C.L., and Victor or Victim, just to name a few.

If you're in any kind of business or want to be a smarter consumer, this book is for you. I couldn't put it down. I haven't found a book this enjoyable in ages. This book is informational and entertaining as well as inspiring. He really makes reading fun again. But, most importantly, I recommend you read it over and over again especially if you want your business to improve and grow.

Andrew Carnegie verbalized the key to real success over one hundred years ago, "The only way you can help anyone is by helping them help somebody." I know this book can help you, but it will become an experience when you share David's wisdom and knowledge.

Charles "Tremendous" Jones
Author of the Best Seller *Life is Tremendous!*
President, ExecutiveBooks.com
Mechanicsburg, Pennsylvania

ACKNOWLEDGEMENTS

To my wife, partner and best friend, *Mary Ellen Brice-Alan*, who is always in my corner through thick and thin and helps keep me on track with her love, caring, hard work and advise. Without you this wouldn't be possible. I love you Honey!

To my mom, *Edith S. Levin*, my other best friend who bestowed to me her positive attitude on life and has always been there for me. You have helped me pick my self up off the ground more time than I can count. I couldn't have made it without you. I love you Mom!

Maurice J. Pitt, my father and hero, who passed when I was only 10 years old. Dad, how I wish you could see and know me now.

To my brother, *Michael H. Pitt*, my sister *Marcia Morgan*, and my Bonus dad, *Dr. Leo J. Levin*.

To my son and golfing buddy, *Thomas Michael Brice*, may you always have the courage to live your dreams.

My friend, *Ronald S. Torch*, who has been like a brother to me my entire life.

Smokey Santillo, a brother, friend and mentor, who has taught me so much about diet, health and life.

Dan Ferante, my printer, who's feedback, advise and friendship have been invaluable.

Hal Becker, my friend, who inspired me to write this book and turned me on to the best publisher in the business.

Master Tao Huang, a brother, whose friendship, support and keen insights are always inspiring and refreshing.

Ed Helvey, the best publisher a writer could have who went above and beyond to help make this book a success.

ADDITIONAL ACKNOWLEDGEMENTS

Don Allan
Don Allen
Lou Aloi
Enzo Armanetti
Russell Z. Baron
W. Craig Bashein
David Belloff*
Cindy Brice
Dolores Brice
Tammy Brice
Steven Byers*
Bob Callahan
Nick Ciani
Grant Cleveland
Robert Cummings
Brianne Dipinto
Laurie Dipinto
Lindsey Dipinto
Michael Dublo
Carl Endreola Jr.
Bruce Fairchild
Eugene Felsen*
Sam Felsen
Brian Finnegan
Paul Flowers
Mark Fogliano
Russell Folisi
Michael Gardner
Joe Garrett
John Girty

Pamela Sue Goldfarb*
Andrea Graley
Kent A. Greenes
Elisha Harris
Tom and Karen Harrison
Steven Hartstein
Denny Hawes*
Susan Haynie
Dorothy Hollander
Hawthorne Valley
    Country Club staff
Charles Kaplan
Wally Kenate
Kenny Kurland
Ihor Lenko
David C. Littlefield
Julie A. Burden-Lindner
Mike Lynam
Jack Madda
Diane Martin
Gino Medaglia
Jeffery Mills
Michael L. Minotti
Martin and Phyllis Mirves
Nick Monticalvo
Nick Montoni
David Morgan
Ronald Mott
Mike Noble
Ron Oostdyk

Jan Orlando
Port Royal Patrons
Simon Peters
Ab Picciuto
Vince Picone
James Pilla
Harold Pitt
Joe Pitt*
Uncle Max Pitt*
Jerry and Ester Posen*
Paul Posen
Steve Posen
Carl Quagliotta
Howard Rabb
Leo Rosner
Russell Scott Rybar*
Dawn Santillo
Humbart Santillo Sr*
Michael Santillo
Dr. Aaron Scheff
Joseph W. Schervish
Nick Sciarabba
Thomas Scully

Bernard and Lois Shepard
Michael Shepard*
Shiya
Rhonda Goldfarb Sigman*
Robert Sigman
Steve Small
N.Lindsey Smith
William E. Spear Jr.
Donn A. Spitzer
James Sullivan
Elliot Sustin
Elsie Sustin
Mark Sustin
Shawna Suta
Brad Thompson
Lil Torch
Mark Torch
Michele Torch
Jim Vella
Sam Vella
Tom Weekley
Kathy Belloff –Weltman
Steve Zapotechne

*Those names with astericks are now deceased.

INTRODUCTION

ALL SUCCESSFUL ENDEAVORS LEAVE CLUES

I've put into this book my clues from over thirty years of business experience. Using these clues, I have generated over $200 million in revenue for a handful of clients in just a few short years.

In those thirty years, I made a lot of money and I lost a lot. I have been broke many times but I never gave up. They say being broke is a temporary economic situation but that being poor is a permanent mindset of your spirit. I totally believe that. The sign in front of my desk which has been there for years reads, "YOU NEVER FAIL UNTIL YOU STOP TRYING." It's all in your mindset.

Even as a little kid, I had a millionaire mindset. Back then I saw myself as a rich, successful businessman. I finally became one but it took opportunity coupled with years of experience. I'm not saying that because of my experience I'm some all-knowing guru but I have acquired enough sense and wisdom from those opportunities and experiences to do what I know works and to avoid what doesn't. Throughout this book, I'll be sharing some of that sense (and a little wisdom) with you.

First, all businesses share some similarities. Some things are the same across the board; some are not. Knowing what to do and what not to do takes experience. People who are already successful in business can tell you some things that will help, regardless of what your business is or what their business is.

Wisdom comes from not only having acquired experience but applying it every day to your own situation. *Nothing is stronger to you than your own unique experiences.*

Throughout this book I'm going to invite you to pull from your own experiences and couple them with the information I'm passing along. *The idea of this book is to combine your experience with some new information to catapult you forward into new, grand, fantastic experiences.* All of these experiences go into what makes up what you call *your life.*

* * *

When I started **MAIL-RITE INTERNATIONAL®** we made a profit from day one and have continued to do so ever since. I purposely don't do many things that most businesses continue to do. I don't take energy away from my major focus. Spending lots of money on big fancy offices, equipment, and support staff are some examples. Expanding too quickly or opening new enterprises without at least a year's worth of cash behind them are two others. Each of these activities leads into trouble down the road. I have been there before (that's my *experience*), and I am never going back.

One of the biggest problems a business can face is the management's ego. Ego must be kept in check or it will check you out! Whether you're a small sole proprietor or a huge conglomerate — whether you've been in business for one year or thirty — an unchecked ego seems to steer a business away from where it needs to be. An unchecked ego thinks, *If I can do this* (whatever *this* is), *then I can do anything.* Time usually proves them wrong. Stay off the ego road. Be careful because it will beckon you many times. Certainly you should try new things but have the sense to stay with what you do best: the thoughts and actions that put you where you are in the first place.

Remember, a huge unchecked ego will ruin you.

Have the sense to take the advice of people who have been there before you and who know what they are talking about, *especially* if these people care about you and want you to succeed. Because of their experience, they know how to make it happen and they'll want to see it happen for you.

HOW TO GET THE MOST
OUT OF THIS BOOK

THIS BOOK IS WRITTEN IN A UNIQUE FORM
MOST OF THE CHAPTERS WILL FOLLOW THIS FORMAT

1) MAJOR STATEMENT IN LARGE TYPE

2) EXPLANATIONS OF MAJOR STATEMENT IN :

A) ADVERTISING & DIRECT MAIL

B) AS IT RELATES TO SALES

C) HOW IT RELATES TO YOUR LIFE

3) STORIES TO EXPLAIN & CLARIFY
(the ideas in that chapter)

4) SPACE FOR YOU TO WRITE YOUR ANSWERS
(each chapter has profound thought provoking questions)

THERE ARE THREE WAYS TO ENJOY THIS BOOK

1) JUST READ THE MAJOR STATEMENTS FROM EACH CHAPTER *(TAKES ONLY 10 MINUTES)*

2) READ EVERYTHING INCLUDING THE 26 STORIES *(TAKES JUST A FEW HOURS)*

3) READ EVERYTHING INCLUDING THE 26 STORIES AND DO THE EXERCISES AT THE END OF EACH CHAPTER *(TAKE AS LONG AS YOU LIKE)*

THIS BOOK

IS WRITTEN

IN THIS

<u>*STYLE*</u>

AND

<u>*FORMAT*</u>

TO RESPECT

<u>*YOUR*</u>

<u>*VALUABLE*</u>

TIME

AND

ENERGY

A MESSAGE FROM THE AUTHOR

I WROTE THIS BOOK ON
WHAT I DO
AND
HOW I FEEL ABOUT...

ADVERTISING,

SALES

And

DIRECT MAIL

BECAUSE ...

I

GET

IT

and . . .

IN ANY PROFESSION

THAT'S

WHAT

COUNTS

!!!

IF
YOU
DON'T
GET
IT

(Your Profession)

DO

YOURSELF

The

FAVOR

and . . .

GET
OUT

then . . .

GET

INTO

SOMETHING

THAT

YOU DO

GET

LIFE'S
TOO SHORT TO
BE
ANYTHING
OTHER THAN
WHAT
YOU WERE
MEANT TO
DO or BE

DO WHAT YOU LOVE

THE REST FALLS IN PLACE

You'll find your bliss wrapped up in something that you love. Become one with that, and there you are.

If you can align yourself with what you love, your work becomes a joy—another reason to wake up in the morning. You will excel in that field of endeavor because it comes naturally to you.

We all have been given talents and abilities. Most of all, we each have been given special gifts in the form of extraordinary talents and abilities, whether it's sports, music, art, being creative, cooking, cleaning, climbing, accounting, business, crafts, even wiggling your ears. If you're not sure what your special talents and abilities are, ask yourself: *What do I do better than anyone else I know? What do I do—or what can I think about—naturally, with little or no effort?* If you still don't know, think about this: *What did I love to do as a child? What were my hobbies and interests? What was I doing when time just flew by?* If you're still having trouble with this line of thought, ask someone who is close to you: *What am I the best at? What special talents do you see that I have?*

If you're still stumped, try these: *If I were on my deathbed, what would I regret never having done or been? What would I do if I knew I could not fail?*

I'm not saying you have to figure out what you can do or where you'd be the best in the world, like a Tiger Woods, Michael Jordan, or Steven Spielberg. Just nail down where you can be the best you that you can be.

Throughout this book I relate stories about the numerous businesses I have owned and the careers I have had. People frequently ask me how I got into the direct mail business. Because a major portion of this book deals with direct mail, the first story comes from that field.

Story One

I was an independent contractor for Craftmatic of Pittsburgh. I sold the Contour chair and the Craftmatic bed. The method of selling these particular items was in-the-home sales. Another name for it was a "one-call close": you either make the sale when you go there or you don't. No return calls. No salary or draw. One hundred percent commission. Eat or starve. I ate and as a matter of fact I did extremely well over a five-year period. For me, the major drawback was that there were no repeat sales. Every day I was starting over, and I finally grew tired of it. I wanted a career that would have a repeat customer base.

In January 1993, I answered an ad for selling advertising to car dealers. The selling method was direct mail. The potential for repeat sales was there. I was hired in February 1993.

The first month was tough because I was in a venue completely different than anything I had ever experienced. When I was with Craftmatic, I was always one of the top salesman, frequently number-one in sales in a four-state region.

As you might imagine, selling to a car dealer is quite a feat. We're talking about some of the toughest, shrewdest businesspeople in the world. I tell people that selling to car dealers is like being in a shark tank. One drop of blood or sign of weakness, and they'll eat you for lunch, bones and all. After being chewed up and spit out for about a month, two options remained: quit, or become a dolphin. I chose the latter. Sharks don't eat dolphins. Sharks respect dolphins and don't eat them.

To me, becoming a dolphin meant:

- Growing a thick skin.
  (Learn not to take rejection personally.)
- Understanding their business and how it works.
  (Sounds easy, but you'd be surprised how many people don't take this approach, no matter the field.)
- Becoming someone they could turn to when they felt hungry.
  (Gain their trust and never take advantage of it.)
- Being able to swim around the sharks and not get bit.
  (Sell by asking, not telling.)
- Swimming along with them.
  (Becoming their ally, not their enemy.)
- Bringing them an incredible amount of food to eat.
  (Having sales that brought them more customers and more sales than anyone else.)
- Finding food for them when everyone else said the cupboard was bare.
  (Providing successful sales where others had failed.)
- Just being a dolphin.
  (Dolphins bring joy wherever they go, and people [even sharks] like being around them.)

After a couple of months, I started writing the ad copy myself, which worked great. Throughout my different businesses and careers, I almost always wrote my own advertising. Ad agencies frequently asked who did my advertising. They were always surprised when I told them I did it myself. *Writing ad copy always came naturally to me, which is why I was good at it—so good that professionals noticed.* I had often wondered in previous years what writing ads would be like as a profession, and that's what I ended up doing. (You never know.)

I had been in this direct-mail-to-car-dealers business for about a year when the company I was working for did me the biggest favor. Actually what they did was, in reality, dishonest. They promised certain benefits and they asked me to purchase things from people I knew that cost thousands of dollars, saying that the company would pay for them. Needless to say, they did neither.

Their bad actions were blessings in disguise, as are many bad things that happen to you. Now I had a situation. I thought a lot about what had happened, and here's what I did:

First, I went to my customers and confided in them and asked , "If I go out on my own, would you go with me?" They all said approximately the same thing: "David, we do business with you. As long as you can provide the same level of service that we've come to know, the answer is yes."

Second, I made arrangements to personally pay the companies from which I had purchased the supplies.

From these two decisions, **MAIL-RITE INTERNATIONAL®** was launched in March 1994 and I have never looked back.

This book is like a

ROLLER COASTER

STIMULATING

INVIGORATING

FUN

Leaving your mind

BURSTING

With

NEW IDEAS

And

REALIZATIONS

So . . .

BUCKLE YOUR SEATBELT YOU'RE GOING FOR A RIDE !!!

CHAPTER ONE

HOW DO YOU RECEIVE NEW KNOWLEDGE?

HOW

DO YOU

RECEIVE

NEW

KNOWLEDGE

?

ARE YOU . . .

LIBERATED

BY IT

OR

ARE YOU

OVERWHELMED

?

I wanted to say <u>crushed</u> but People said that was too strong

Your answer to this question determines how much you're going to get out of this book, and life for that matter. If learning liberates, invigorates, and inspires you, you're going to have a ball. If you don't like to learn new things—you hate change and acquiring new knowledge makes you feel *overwhelmed*—you shouldn't, frankly, expect great results.

Change is not easy. *Great things are only accomplished by implementing massive change through knowledge followed by action.* Implementing is a really important word here. If you have knowledge and don't implement it (meaning you don't act on it or use it), it's like you're planning a great trip around the world and never leaving the house. You're not going very far or accomplishing anything great.

Understanding how we learn can help in implementing new knowledge. Consider the following concepts, which I learned from a great sales trainer and author, Tom Hopkins.

The Four Stages of Knowledge and Learning

Unconscious Incompetence—You have no idea that you don't know what you're doing.

Conscious Incompetence—You now realize that you don't know what you're doing.

Conscious Competence—You have taken in new knowledge, and you're trying to implement it. You must concentrate, however, and keep vigilant so that you can accomplish whatever it is you're doing right.

Unconscious Competence—You use your new knowledge correctly without having to think about it. You do it right automatically.

To give you an example of these concepts in action, think back to when you were learning how to drive. . . .

Unconscious Incompetence—You sit behind the wheel and think it's going to be easy. You have yet to realize that you stink as a driver.

Conscious Incompetence—You now realize this driving thing isn't as easy as it looks. You have to concentrate and do many things at once. You're *overwhelmed*, and you wonder if you'll ever figure everything out.

Conscious Competence—Driving is hard but you're starting to get the hang of it. You can't take your mind off what you're doing for a second but now you are driving okay.

Unconscious Competence—Driving is a breeze. You feel *liberated*. Now you can drive one-handed, listen to the radio, talk on the phone, and sightsee all at the same time without even thinking about it. You now know that you know how to drive!

Stages two and three on this knowledge and learning scale are the most uncomfortable because you feel the friction and are totally aware of what's transpiring—whether it's good or bad. Realize as we go forward into this book that practicing and implementing the concepts, skills, and ideas in here may take some time. The most important thing for now is to *relax*. Most of what we'll be talking about is fun and easy to learn.

Let's get busy.

CHAPTER TWO

OPEN THE ENVELOPE
OR ELSE

OP

TH

ENVE

Or

EN

E

LOPE

else …

THAT'S

NOTH

IT'S

Now go back and re-read to derive the <u>hidden</u> <u>meaning</u>

RIGHT

ING!!

OVER

*these last 6 pages, 3 more times
and keep rereading it <u>until</u> <u>you</u> <u>get</u> <u>it</u>.*

OUR
ENVELOPES
ARE

PHENO

THAT _EVEN_
WHO HANDLE

ARE _ALWAYS_
INTO OPEN

Does everyone open the enve

& PACKAGES

SO

MENAL

<u>THE</u> <u>VENDORS</u>

OUR MAIL

<u>MISDIRECTED</u>

ING THEM

lopes of mail that you send?

DO YOUR

SCR

HEY…

THROW

Ask ten people who <u>are</u> <u>not</u>

"If you received this letter in

If you're not getting at least 7 out of

ENVELOPES

EAM?

I'M JUNK!!!

ME AWAY

in your area or department:

the mail, would you open it?"

10 to say yes, start your envelope over.

Direct Mail

The *envelope* is the wrapper. Just like you'd wrap a present. What really counts is what's on the inside of the package, but if you don't do a good job at wrapping the package, you won't create the desire to open it.

How much hard work and creativity did you spend on the *inside* of the envelope, on the *contents*? What about the money it cost to produce? Even if you're giving away hundred-dollar bills, if the envelopes you send don't get opened, your hundred-dollar bills will be thrown away. The contents are never seen and everything you did was for nothing. That's what happens when your envelopes aren't opened.

Have you ever stopped to think about how much time and money you waste when only 50 percent of your envelopes or packages are opened? What you want to focus on is ensuring that your envelopes have a *95 percent open rate.*

How do you do that? Keep reading.

The envelope needs to mean something to the recipient, good or bad. Your recipients must be enticed or scared into opening the envelope. They'll want to open that envelope, whether with anticipation or out of fear. *Every action a person makes is either to gain pleasure or avoid pain.* That concept is known as the *pleasure-pain principle,* and if you can use that principle correctly, the recipients will open your envelopes. Think about it: you have to use the principle. Just knowing about it and not using it is like planning that round-the-world trip and not leaving home.

Whatever you do, though, don't telegraph your moves. Don't send a signal of what you're going to do before you do it. Remember the saying, "Don't let the cat out of the bag."

What happens if a boxer telegraphs his punches? Right—he's knocked out! Imagine if a quarterback tells the defense right before he snaps the ball, "We're going to throw a bomb in the end zone." What do you think his chances are of ever completing that touchdown pass? Not very good. Then why would you let the recipient of your letter or package know what's inside before they open it? In other words, as the late great sales trainer David Sandler said, *"Don't spill your popcorn in the lobby."*

Story Two

I had been doing business with my printer for about five years. During that time, he had printed millions of mail pieces for me.

One day I get a phone call from him saying, "You @!*!#()*^. You almost gave me a heart attack."

I said, "What are you talking about?"

He said, "I just got one of your mailers and I thought I was getting sued! Then I opened it up and saw it was from you."

"Gotcha!" I said, laughing.

"Can you believe it?" he said. "And here, I was the one who printed it" (not the envelope, the contents).

Speaking of contents, *what about your own contents?* Your own potential? How much is locked up inside of you? **What would your life be like if you opened your own envelope and let the greatness out?** Maybe your life could be everything you've ever dreamed of? Do you ever think about that?

Story Three

We were having some difficulties with delivery in one of the cities where my mail was going. Some of the executives of that city's post office offered to be seeded (which means they were going to be mailed the same letters we were mailing to the consumer to see if and when they received that mail piece). Now keep in mind they had been shown what types of mailers I was mailing. In this way, they could recognize the piece when it came in. I let them know, however, that I would be changing the envelopes periodically so that the consumer would not recognize my mail. (*Never mail the same look twice to the same people in a twelve-month period.*)

At the meeting at the post office, one of the women postal executives said, "Before this meeting starts, I have a story to tell." Seems that the other day her teenage daughter called her at work, frantic. The postal exec said, "What's wrong?" The daughter said, "We got this letter in the mail and I think someone's suing us!" The postal executive, now nervous herself, told her daughter to open the letter immediately and read it to her. Now both of them are nervous while the envelope is being opened. Then the daughter exclaims, "Mom, it's from that car dealer again! It's an advertisement". Needless to say, the mail was from me. The postal executive was telling this story with a smile on her face and with admiration for the ingenuity of an envelope that caused such a fuss.

By the way, all of my envelopes do not look like they came from an attorney. Actually, very few do, but you'll never know. Maybe one day you can tell the story of how this guy who wrote a book you read fooled you into opening the envelope, too.

Sales

What business opportunities are waiting for you to open and explore? Have you picked up the phone and made those cold calls that would start the sales process? Did you step out of the comfort of your office or your car and make those cold sales calls? What about your warm sales calls and referrals? What are you doing about them? Did you return the phone calls that you know you should but you're afraid to? (Welcome to the club!)

We all procrastinate and are afraid. Some of us just become accustomed to it. You should face your fears constantly so that eventually they become no big deal. Making these calls should be like calling back a friend. When you call a friend, you don't sit there with your palms sweating and afraid to pick up the phone. You just pick up the phone and call with a positive expectation, not a negative one.

What about that company or executive you're afraid to approach because you think they're too big or important? Maybe you feel that you're not important enough to talk to them (so you think).

We're all afraid of rejection. You'll learn, though, that *working through and overcoming this fear is your road to living and exploring your dreams.*

Story Four

Back in 1978, I had enough of the cold winters in Cleveland, Ohio, especially after the famous blizzards of 1977 and 1978. In 1978, I decided to move to Tucson, Arizona. My good friend Sam and his dad had shown me the basics of being a locksmith, and I decided to move there and open up my own shop (a mere 120 square feet, a 10-by-12-foot room). Between late

1978 and early 1979, I made two trips to Tucson to set everything up. I sold most of the things I owned and invested my money in locksmith equipment and locks. In May 1979, I drove twenty-five hundred miles to my new life.

My cousin Kent lived in Tucson, and fortunately I made a few new friends through him. I also didn't have much money left and if I was going to eat and survive I had to start working fast.

I read a great book by the famous car salesman Joe Girard, *"How To Sell Anything to Anyone"*. In his book, he relayed his three-foot rule: Hand anybody that's within three feet of you a business card and tell them what you do. I took his advice and *handed out seven thousand cards in six weeks*. I would stop cars at traffic lights. I'd go in every store and shop I could see. I would even go to malls and stop shoppers and say, "Hi, I'm David Alan. I'm a locksmith and if you ever need one here's my card." There wasn't a day that I went out that I didn't get a lead or a job when I followed that procedure.

I built the fastest-growing locksmith company in southern Arizona. Within five years I was one of the biggest in the entire state. By 1983, we were averaging a minimum of one hundred people in my store a day. Sometimes the store would be so crowded that the people would fill the showroom and start a line that would wrap part way around the building. (Now, though, the store was thirty-six hundred square feet, fifteen employees, seven vehicles, and five phone lines ringing off the wall.) We even explored having a take-a-number system installed to help take care of the crowds.

One day in 1984 one of my counter people came to me and said, "There's a guy out here that has a card he says you gave him five years ago in a mall, but I don't recognize the card." (Over the five years I had revamped and restyled our cards and logo numerous times as the company evolved.) Sure enough the card was one of the ones I gave out when I first started. This gentleman had kept it in his wallet for five years until he needed it. As I told my counter man, "See? You never know who or when someone will need your services. That's why you tell everyone you can what you do and give them a card." What if I had never opened the envelope of Tucson? What if I knew about Joe Gerard's advice and never did anything with it? For starters, I wouldn't have this story to tell or the incredible experiences that went with it.

Life

Have you been meaning to call someone? Someone you've been meaning to tell that you love them? A friend? A lover? A parent? A mentor? Is there something you've been meaning to do, to start, to complete? How about something as simple as "I'm sorry" or "I forgive you." Maybe the time has come to mend old fences or just to tear down something that doesn't work or fit into your life anymore.
What have you been putting off that will change your life but will never happen unless you open its envelope? What needs to be opened up in your life? Think!

I want you to stop reading right now and make a list of what envelopes need to be opened in your life. Are you afraid of what you might find? Come on! You're tough enough. You wouldn't have come this far if you weren't. It's okay. I'll wait for you to come back before we continue.

LIST OF WHAT NEEDS TO BE OPENED
UP IN MY LIFE RIGHT NOW

(Just write, right now without judging yourself or your choices. Let it flow freely.)

Story Five

One of the best and most important envelopes I ever opened in my life was on Thanksgiving Eve 1992. The weather was cold, and I was heading home from an appointment. I drove by my friend David's house and saw a few cars in his driveway, so I stopped in.

"What's going on?" I said.

"We're going out for Thanksgiving Eve."

I asked why.

"Because it's the biggest bar night of the year". (I was thirty-seven years old and had been going to bars since I was seventeen, and I didn't know that. You learn something new every day.)

My friend David said, "Why don't you come out with us?"

"When are you leaving?" I said. He said in about forty-five minutes. "Why not?" I said, so I rushed home, changed, and came right back.

Sure enough, downtown was a zoo—people were everywhere. The night was unbelievable and I was having a blast. I saw people I hadn't seen in ages. After a couple of hours and a few places they said, "Okay, now it's time to head back to our neighborhood to a place called the Swamp Club."

We walked in and I couldn't believe what I was seeing: wall-to-wall people. Hundreds of them packed in like sardines.

I was standing in the middle of this place when I spotted this beautiful blonde (she had her eyes all scrunched up because, as I found out later, she was looking for her sister and didn't have her glasses on). I said, "Smile." She looked at me, smiled, and muttered something under her breath that I can't repeat here. The Swamp Club was so crowded that after a while I went next door to MiMi's with my friend Michael Shepard just so I could breathe.

When I came back to the Swamp Club an hour or so later, the crowd had thinned out a little, but not much. I kept seeing that blonde, though, and I wanted to talk to her. I knew that after the first encounter, I couldn't walk up to her without a reason. I kept my eyes open and looked for an opportunity to present itself. Sure enough, one came along. I saw a friend of mine who was a hairdresser talking with her so I made my move.

"Hey, Enzo. How are you doing, and who's your friend?" That was all I needed. I moved in front of him and started talking with her. We talked for hours. By the way, she's now my wife. We've been together ever since.

If I hadn't opened this envelope, I wouldn't be with the women of my dreams, let alone have married her. I used Enzo as the letter opener.

Remember that finding and asking for help is okay. Look what it did for me.

How many envelopes of opportunity did I open?

I stopped by my friend's house.

I decided to go out.

I kept an open mind.

I looked for the opportunity.

I grabbed it when I saw the opening.

And that's just in a few hours. Think what you can do over a lifetime if you just open the envelopes. *But you have to start.*

Moral of the Stories

Whether we're talking about direct mail, sales, or even personal relationships, life is always unfolding right before your eyes, prompting you to open its envelopes. You'll never know what's waiting around the corner unless you open those envelopes.

Now It's Time for Your Story

What stories in your life have I triggered or reminded you of? Times when you opened up an important envelope? Write them down right here, right now.

Remember: *Nothing is more powerful to you than your own experiences.*

Your Stories

Now take the list you wrote earlier regarding envelopes you should open and combine that with your list of the important envelopes you opened in your own life. Ask yourself: How can I use this information and these combined experiences in my business or life right now?

Write down the answers before you go to the next chapter.

CHAPTER THREE

REASONS FOR A SALE

What do these 5 reasons for a sale have in common?

SALE   SALE   SALE

GRAND OPENING

30 YEAR ANNIVERSARY

INVENTORY REDUCTION

GOING OUT OF BUSINESS

Y.C.C.

YOUR CUSTOMER

ALL THEY <u>CARE</u>

C.L.

COULD CARE LESS

ABOUT <u>IS</u> ...

W. I. I.

WHAT'S IN

ME   ME

If you don't <u>tune</u>
I guarantee they'll

F. M

IT FOR ME?

ME   ME

into their station,
turn off yours!!!

Advertising and Direct Mail: Having a Reason for a Sale

Companies think that their reason for having a sale is the same reason that the customer should care or want to come in their store.

NEWS FLASH: Customers don't care, and the reasons aren't the same. Customers don't care why you're having a sale. They only care about what's in it for them, period. The only exception for when they *might* really care is if they know you personally, like a relative or close friend.

Imagine that you're sitting at a lunch counter and a stranger says to you, "I got a raise and a promotion today." Do you really care? As a fellow human being you might think, *that's nice.* Then your next thought would probably be, *Hmmm, maybe he'll buy lunch.* If not, then you'll probably just move on to asking him to pass the salt. You don't really care.

If that little scenario makes sense to you then I have a question.

Why *would* a perfect stranger care why you're having a sale? Aren't most of your new potential customers strangers? Are you starting to see my point?

So many companies quote slogans and have sales that flatter their own egos but these slogans and sales mean nothing to the consumer. So what happens? While a company's ego is getting a boost, sales fall flat. Then the company's managers scratch their heads and wonder why their sales didn't work.

When I look at most of the sales ads out there today, I want to vomit. The ads stink and the consumer knows it. The advertisers, though, don't have a clue.

Consider the line, "We're overstocked so we must make room for our new inventory." That line is so old it should be collecting Social Security. *Wouldn't it be refreshing if companies told the truth?* How about, "We goofed and bought too much stuff. Now we have to discount everything or lose our shirts. Capitalize on our misfortune because we're not making that mistake again. Once was enough, so come on in." This company could even say they're running a "learning curve sale." At least the company would be giving a valid reason that makes sense to the consumer. All the customers need to know is that they'll be benefiting from your mistake. *Remember: Customers don't care about you. They care about themselves.*

Story Six

I mentioned before that one of my specialties is doing direct mail for car dealers. Most car ads that I see have too much mumbo-jumbo in them. Open the car section of any big city newspaper to see what I mean. Back in 1994, when I started **MAIL-RITE INTERNATIONAL®**, I wanted to be different. I looked at why people buy cars and the selling process. What I found was that people really only want a few things when they buy a car. These few things are each consumer's "hot buttons." Among a car buyer's hot buttons are:

1) Big money for their trade-in (even if it's worth ten cents)
2) They want to pay nothing for the new car
3) They don't want the dealer to make ten cents
4) Their payment shouldn't be more than a dollar a month (and that's too much).

Believe it or not, those four points summarize most car buyer's feelings. If you don't believe me, show this list to any car dealer and see if they don't laugh and agree.

In the real world, we all know that the car business couldn't run this way but people think and hope that it can. Customers have a few more hot buttons, but we'll cover those in future chapters.

Based on those hot buttons, I designed a phenomenal Direct Mail piece. That mail piece and ones like it have helped to sell thousands of cars, trucks, vans and sport utility vehicles, generating tens of millions of dollars.

Regarding the rule that no one cares about the reason for a sale, there is one exception: If you're going to use a reason for a sale, the reason must tie into the sale. In other words, *the reason for the sale must be the reason that the consumer wants to buy.*

Story Seven

One of my car dealers was having its thirtieth anniversary. The son of the dealer asked me if I could come up with a sale to celebrate the anniversary. The interesting thing about this dealership was that it was owned by a set of identical twins. The twins had slowly bought into this business over a few years until they owned 100 percent of it. They had now owned it for thirty years and as a family business it was very successful. They may have been the only set of twins to own a major car dealership, but I'm not sure. One of the national trade magazines thought so and wrote an article on the twins and their thirty-year anniversary. It was a great article, the kind that most people find interesting and charming.

Armed with all that information I came up with a devastating Direct Mail program. I reproduced the article for inclusion in every mailer because people love nostalgia (the article also had some old pictures of the twins advertising their cars).

Then I designed a letter telling about the thirty-year anniversary. I tied everything together by offering every new car for only thirty dollars over invoice. The results were fantastic. This sale was the best sale they have ever had in thirty years. Consequently, on their thirty-fifth anniversary we did it again with a thirty-five-dollar-over-invoice sale, and that sale's record beat the one from the thirtieth anniversary.

Sales: Tying in Your Reason

People buy for their own reasons not yours. How many times have you had a salesperson say to you, "If I get one more sale this month, I'll win a trip," or "I get a special TV prize"? Hearing this, don't you say to yourself, *Who cares, unless you're taking us with you,* or *If we help you win a TV, we want one too.*

Remember Y.C.C.L.: *"Your customer could care less."* Could you imagine your doctor saying, "If I do one more gallbladder operation this month my family gets a trip to Europe!" Does that make you want to run right out and have your gallbladder removed? Of course not, primarily because the doctor is not being professional. Now, if you said the same thing as a salesperson (and again I don't recommend it because it's not professional for you either) except now you said, "If I make this sale, I win a trip . . . and if I win that trip, you folks get another 20 percent off," that sale has changed the same approach around to our concept of W. I. I. F. M *"What's in it for me?"*

Story Eight

In 1996, my fiancée (now my wife) and I went looking for a dining room set. We wanted a light color. In the northeast part of the country, a light-colored dining room set is really hard to find. Every store we went to had lots of dark or medium-color wood dining room sets, but they carried only one or two, if any, light colored sets. Our frustration and exhaustion were mounting.

We were in this big furniture store when we found what we thought was a nice light-colored dining room set. Then I sat down in one of the chairs, it felt like an old park bench. Like most people, I value comfort in my furniture. When I told the salesman it was really uncomfortable, he said, "That's okay. You'll sit down and eat, then as soon as you're done you get up." *Sure*, I thought, *as long as you make your sale, what does it matter if we're satisfied with your product?* Needless to say we were out of there in the blink of an eye. The self-centered, incompetent salesperson probably wondered why we left.

I don't know about you, but our dining room was going to be used mostly when we were entertaining. How would you like if you went to someone's house for dinner and as soon as you were done eating the host said, "Is everyone really uncomfortable? Good, then let's retire to the living room"? Then everyone would get up, bent over in agony, grunting and groaning. . . . I don't think so. Most people like to spend time at the dining room table, eating and talking when they have guests over. I know we do. That salesman didn't care what we wanted. Just as long as he made the sale. Guess what? He didn't.

How many times have you experienced something like that? Probably more times than you could count. Let me ask you something. Did you like it? Then why would you do that to someone who needs or wants your goods or services? Hopefully you don't. Not if you want more business, and who doesn't want that?

Life: A Reason for the Sale

Maybe you need some personal-life sales. I recommend three types of personal-life sales.

> *Toxic sales*
> *Positive-attribute exchange sales*
> *Outgrew it or can't use it sales*

One of the spiritual laws in the physical and nonphysical realms of life is that you can't acquire something new unless you let go of or give up something that you have, especially if it doesn't fit or enhance your life anymore. In other words (using baseball as the metaphor), you can't steal nor be on second base with your foot still on first, and you'll never get to home unless you cover (touch) all the bases. Are you stuck on first? What bases aren't you covering?

What's a Toxic Sale?

A *toxic sale* rids yourself of all the toxic habits, people, and circumstances in your life. Sorry to say, we simply need to let toxic people go. (I never said this process was easy.) My definition of toxic is anyone or anything that is not a positive influence in your life. You might even like the toxic people in your life. We indulge lots of people and circumstances in our lives that we know are not good for us, and these toxic people and circumstances hold us back. They do not propel us forward.

How do you know if something or someone is toxic? Ask yourself these questions. Do you feel better or worse when you're around them? Do you feel energized or drained after you've been with them? You may even be comfortable around these people, but how do you feel when they're gone? I can feel comfortable (for a short time) around certain people, but for the most part life has made them bitter and they are not a positive influence on me. Are they into self-destructive activities like drugs, excessive drinking, and partying? Are they all about keeping up with the Joneses, talking bad about other people and jealousy? Are they growing as people? Do you share values with them? Are they doing and going in the direction of life that you are? If not, cut the cord now! What if they're a family member or a coworker? Wean yourself away from them. Cut back on how much time you spend with them. They can only hold you back. Having a toxic sale is for your own good

Remember: I never said it was easy.

What's a Positive Attribute Exchange Sale?

In a positive attribute exchange sale, you exchange negative habits and attributes for positive ones.

The first exchange is having and wanting better health.

On the physical plane, you can't acquire better health unless you give up detrimental physical things like smoking, drugs, excessive alcohol, bad dieting habits (overeating, undereating, and eating the wrong foods), and bad exercise habits (improper exercise and not exercising at all).

The second exchange is having and wanting better habits.

One example of picking up better habits involves smoking. When you give up smoking, think of the exchanges you make:

- Smokers' breath exchanged for sweeter saliva and breath
- Smelling like an ashtray exchanged for not smelling offensive
- Waking up in the morning with that lousy smokers' taste in your mouth exchanged for just morning breath. (not that your breath smells wonderful in the morning, but it's sure a whole lot better)

- Coughing and hacking up parts of your lungs and stomach exchanged for just breathing normally
- Shortened life expectancy and lower quality of life exchanged for having all-around better health and hopefully a longer life

When you change your eating habits, some of the exchanges you make are

- Overeating exchanged for staying slim or not growing fat or fatter
- Having an overstuffed bloated feeling exchanged for leaving the table feeling comfortable
- Looking emaciated exchanged for looking vibrant
- Being stuffed because you ate everything in sight and you're still feeling hungry and unsatisfied exchanged for eating the proper amount and the right foods and now you feel great
- Feeling like an overstuffed sausage and not being able to fit into your clothes exchanged for looking and feeling great in your clothes

By now you should see the point here. With smoking, eating, and exercise, everyone knows the right things to do. But as I said at the beginning of the book, having knowledge is useless unless you put it into action. But given that we've already covered smoking and eating, let's lay it on the line for exercise, too.

If you're not exercising, you should start. If you are exercising already, make sure it's the right kind for you. How do you know what the right kind of exercise is? First, exercise should make you feel better, not worse. Now I'm not saying you won't initially experience some fatigue or discomfort. If you start spraining parts of your body, or after a few weeks you're not either enjoying what you chose or feeling better, then switch exercises. Heavy-duty weightlifting, combat martial arts, and aerobics are not for everyone, especially if you're over thirty-five years old. Personally I recommend choosing one or a few of the following calmer, low-impact exercises: walking, swimming, stretching, light weightlifting, deep breathing, yoga, tai chi, Aikido, and qi gong. *The best exercises are the ones where you feel your best when you do them, and you do them consistently.* Studies show that the majority of people who stick with their exercise program do their exercising first thing in the morning, before life gets in the way to sidetrack them from their exercise routine.

What's an Outgrew-It-or-Can't-Use-It Sale?

This sale is for anything you don't use anymore, whether its things, thoughts, people, or activities. We've already covered some of this subject, but basically you need to clear out from your life whatever no longer has any use to you. An absolutely fabulous book on the subject is *"Clear Your Clutter with Feng Shui"* by Karen Kingston. The book is a fun and easy read that is hard to put down.

What experiences has this chapter reminded you of? Write them down right here, right now before you go on to the next chapter.

Now ask yourself, and write down the answers, What am I holding on to? What am I rationing out or not giving freely? My time? My love? My support? My guidance? How about my possessions or my money?

Now write down how you can use your experiences and this new knowledge coupled with these lists to improve on your business, your relationships, and your life right now.

CHAPTER FOUR

THE BEST TIME FOR A SALE

THE

BEST

TIME

FOR

A

SALE

FOR

MAXIMUM

EFFECTIVENESS

AND

PROFIT . . .

Is...

Either right after you've had a

Successful sale

and/or

In the peak

of your

Month

or

Season

If you were a bear hunter

(and I'm not saying you should be)

Would you go hunting

When the bears are

Hibernating

and

Out of

Season?

Well . . . Would You?

PULL THE

WHEN

TARGET IS IN

AND

THE DUCKS

TRIGGER

YOUR

YOUR SIGHTS

ARE FLYING

IT'S A <u>REAL</u>

TIME &

<u>INSISTING</u> <u>ON</u>

SHOVE A

IN

A SQUARE

Now <u>Go</u> <u>Back</u> to the <u>Duck</u>

<u>WASTE</u> OF

MONEY

<u>TRYING</u> TO

ROUND PEG

HOLE

<u>Statement</u> and <u>Read</u> it <u>Again</u>

Advertising and Direct Mail

Like life, every business goes through cycles or seasons. Knowing your cycles and seasons—as they relate to the best time of the month, week, or day—is very important. This knowledge comes into play whether you are trying to take the best advantage of your life, your body, or your circumstances, and even when your doing business and trying to have a successful sale. If you fight the cycles instead of going with them, you'll most assuredly lose or at best have dismal results.

The first things you need to know for this chapter to be helpful are
> Your on-peak seasons, cycles, or times
> Your off-peak seasons, cycles, or times

Why is knowing your off-times important? Because if you don't know when your downtimes are, you'll always be frustrated, perplexed, and unprofitable. Here's what I mean.

So many people and companies try to force people, circumstances, and the market.

NEWS FLASH: You can't force people, circumstances, or the market.

If you try to force people, circumstances, and the market, most probably you'll experience a dismal failure with unsatisfactory, frustrating results.

I see this over and over again in the marketplace. A company or industry goes through a certain time when business is flat, and yet they insist on trying to make something BIG happen during those times. (I'm not saying you should close your doors during your off-times, although in some industries that's exactly what they do, and that approach is right for them.) However, when companies try to force the market and it doesn't work (and it usually doesn't), management gets upset, yet they continue to try and force their circumstances. Let me ask you a question: When you put your hand on a hot stove a second time and you burn it again, are you surprised?

Story Nine

One of my dealers was having tremendous results with my Direct Mail sales. They would run a four-day sale at the end of each month. (The end of the month is a car dealer's best time to run a sale). This pattern had been going on for over a year with great success. One day my dealer came to me and asked if we could do a four-day sale at the beginning of the month. I strongly recommended against it because nine out of ten times the car business is flat in the first week of every month and sometimes the second week too.

(If you want to know the reasons for these cycles in the car business, visit my Web site: *www.100Milliondollar.com.*)

My client insisted on the beginning-of-the-month sale, so we went ahead. Sure enough, it flopped. He called me up saying how these sales don't work anymore and he'll have to find something new to replace our previous successful sales. Keep in mind that I had recommended against this particular sale, but for the moment his memory failed and all he could see was that my great sales didn't work anymore. Thank goodness we still had another four-day end-of-the-month sale scheduled.

I told my dealer to be patient and that the sale would work again at the end of the month. Anticipating a negative response to the beginning-of-the-month mailer, I had ordered a list and split it evenly in half. The first half was used at the beginning of the month, and the remainder for the end-of-the-month sale. We also used the same exact mail piece. With this approach, we could see the results of the exact same product at different times of the month.

Sure enough, the month-end sale worked great, and my client was a believer again. He also now understood what I had been telling him about trying to force the market and how crucial the timing of a sale is. He said, "I wouldn't have believed it if I hadn't seen completely opposite results with the same people and the same mail piece." Needless to say, he doesn't try to force the market anymore. That was five years ago, and he still does business with me every month.

Story Ten

About a year ago one of my clients called me to say he was at a new dealership and he wanted to do a sale. "Great," I said, until I found out what he wanted. He was the dealership's finance manager, and I had designed a program for him at his last job that had worked tremendously. He wanted the same program as before, except for one difference: first week of the month. When I told him it would not work, he said, "Don't worry. We're going to do two sales every month and I want to get started right now." I asked him if his boss was aware of what I said regarding the first week of the month being a bad time for direct mail auto sales, and he said yes, everything is okay. *Just do the sale.*

Need I tell you what happened? The results were mediocre; they sold some cars and they made some money, but not as much as they wanted. Here's the kicker. His boss knew nothing about what I had said. Consequently, not only did they not do the other sale scheduled for that month, they never did another sale with me again.

Sometimes we need a wakeup call. That experience was one of mine. I knew better but went ahead anyway. Now I refuse all promotions that I feel won't work. Why? Because I would rather lose a single job (short-term gain) than to be part of a failure (long-term loss).

Postscript: After these experiences, I created a mailer for car dealers that works in the first part of the month. Called **BIRTHDAY PREZZENTZ**™. It's a specially designed birthday card that brings people in on their birthday to buy a car. The mailer works great! We also have **BIRTHDAY PREZZENTZ**™ designed to bring people into restaurants and retail stores for one reason: to have fun and spend lots of money.

Sales

The best time to make a sale is right after you just made one. If you've been in sales for any length of time, you have probably experienced the two opposites: being on a roll or being in a slump. When you're on a roll, nothing can stop you. Everyone wants to buy from you, you feel great, and making a sale is easy. When you're in a slump, no one wants to buy from you, you feel lousy, and you couldn't sell a life raft to a drowning man. So what's the answer?

Timing really boils down to your mindset, your core beliefs and your self-image. How you think about yourself and how you think people will react to you and your offer have a great deal of impact on your success. Of course, having a good competitively priced product is important, but that's only a part of it. The biggest part is you.

I think Zig Ziglar said it best when he said, "Your business isn't out there. It's in *here* between your two ears, and if your thinkin' is stinkin', so will your business".

What if you're in a slump? How do you get out of it? You sell your way out by going back to the basics. You read, study, listen to tapes, and keep doing presentations.

Find out what you're doing right and doing wrong. If you're achieving positive results with something, keep doing it. If adverse results are coming your way, change what you're doing. Have a plan and work it. Don't keep winging it; that's what amateurs do.

When's the best time to call or try and sell that tough prospect, the one you want but you're afraid to approach? You guessed it: *right after you just made a sale. Don't wait, do it now while the momentum is in your favor.*

Life

Slash your hatred, mark down your grudges, and give your love away! The time is now! Tomorrow is promised to no one.

Story Eleven

This story—unlike the others which are upbeat—is a tragedy. At the time of writing this section, I have just started writing again after a four-week hiatus. One of my dearest and closest friends of twenty-three years fell over dead of a massive heart attack. His name was Michael Shepard. He had everything going for him—a self-made man who had wealth, love, and happiness. Most of all, he thought he had his health and a long joyful life in front of him. Michael always had this big grin on his face, like the cat that ate the canary. When he came into a room you knew it, and so did every one else. He always wanted to have fun. Over the years I can't tell you how many times he had me crawling on my hands and knees laughing hysterically, tears running down my face, holding my sides in pain yelling, "Stop, stop, I can't breathe."

If you saw him, you would have thought he was a movie star. He looked like Pierce Brosnan, except on a scale of one to ten, Pierce is an eight and Michael was a ten. The day he died he could have been on the cover of a men's health magazine with the caption "45 still looking and feeling great."

Michael was on vacation at a beautiful resort in Phoenix, Arizona. He was with his wife Janet and their two small children. They were having a ball. Michael was an avid golfer and ecstatic because a few days before he had just played the best golf of his life. The day they were supposed to leave the resort and come home they were running a few minutes behind. Michael told his wife he would finish packing a few things in the car and meet her and the kids in front of the resort. The plan was to take back the rental car, catch their plane, and come home.

When Janet came to the front of the resort she didn't see Michael. All she saw was a lot of rental cars that all looked alike except for one with the trunk open. She went over to that one and saw their luggage in the trunk but no Michael. Some people were pointing to the driver's side of the car. When she looked over there, Michael was on the ground, gone. I don't think he knew what hit him. One thing for sure, he thought he had lots of time left on this earth. Unfortunately he didn't know, and neither do most of us.

Don't wait for anything. If there is something you want to say, do, or be, do it now! *Tomorrow is promised to no one, and today could be your last!* **MAKE IT A MASTERPIECE.**

Has this chapter reminded you of any experiences in your life? Write them down right here, right now before you go on to the next chapter.

Write down now: What would you do if you knew you only had one year to live, a month to live and a week to live? Make three separate lists.

Write down now: How can I use my experiences coupled with this new knowledge and these three lists to improve on my business, relationships and life right now?

CHAPTER FIVE

YOUR TARGET IS EVERYTHING

<u>YOUR</u>

TARGET

IS

<u>EVERYTHING</u>

(well . . . almost)

REMEMBER

THE

<u>SMART</u>

BOMBS

OF

DESERT STORM?

The Six Questions

WHO ?

WHAT ?

WHEN ?

WHERE ?

HOW ?

WHY ?

<u>DO</u>

YOUR

DUE

<u>DILIGENCE</u>

I was going to say, "Do your homework,"
but I never met anyone who liked homework.

IT

<u>PAY</u>

HUGE DIV

THAT <u>YOU</u>

YET

IMA

WILL

YOU

IDENDS

HAVE

TO

GINE

Advertising and Direct Mail

When you were a kid did you ever play Pin-the-Tail-on-the-Donkey? Remember how they would blindfold you, then spin you around and let you go? When you took the blindfold off to see where you had pinned the tail, you were lucky if you were even on the correct wall, let alone precisely on target. Unfortunately, a great deal of advertising is performed in the same fashion. In advertising, this approach is called the "shotgun effect," and you're lucky if you hit anything at all.

The problem is usually not the media but how the media is used.

Take billboards for example. In Cleveland, I-480 is a highly traveled freeway that runs east and west. Tens of thousands of cars travel it each day. What types of billboards might you see along that stretch of highway?

A good example of using that media in that location would be something that most or all of those drivers can use: tires. Whether your car is new or used, anyone can get a flat and need a new tire. If you're driving that freeway every day, guess what's getting worn out? Right, your tires. One hundred percent of the people driving on I-480 at some point will be in the market for a tire.

On a totally opposite part of the spectrum, jewelry stores lease billboards for the purpose of advertising an all gold Rolex Submariner watch, which costs over twenty thousand dollars. Less than 1 percent of the population can even *think* of affording that watch, and not all of that 1 percent would even consider buying one. Ninety-nine percent of the people driving on I-480 cannot buy that watch, even if they wanted to.

I'm not saying that advertising a Rolex watch is wrong, or even that anything is wrong with advertising it on a billboard. But wouldn't that money be better spent on media that target the 1 percent who can afford the Rolex Submariner watch, instead of the 99 percent who can't?

The Rolex billboard is an example of what we talked about earlier in the book: ego running rampant. Lots of advertisers and agencies are caught up in where their advertising is as it pertains to status and ego. With this type of advertising purchase, the agency can boast about *where* they advertise, instead of *how* they advertise as it pertains to the right media for the best results.

Advertising of any kind is a percentage and odds game. Do you want the odds to be stacked for you or against you? If you want the odds stacked heavily against you, go to Las Vegas or Atlantic City. They'll be happy to take your money. If you want the odds stacked in your favor, which means to have a better chance of making money, maybe a better bet would be targeting your advertising to the right people (the ones who have the ability or need for your product or service), instead of splattering your ad all over the place and hoping that maybe the right people see it.

Your target is everything. Before you spend your money on advertising, you should ask yourself the six questions that people in journalism school learn on Day One: *Who, What, When, Where, How,* and *Why*.

Let's pose these six questions as they pertain to Direct Mail or advertising:

- *Who* is your customer? *Who* is going to do your promotion?

- *What* products are you going to use for the ad, or *what* products do you want to sell? *What* is your reason for having a sale in the first place?

- *When* is the best time to have a promotion? *When* are your customers most likely to buy?

- *Where* are your customers coming from? *Where* do you need your pricing to be for your promotion to entice them to buy, and then actually make the purchase?

- *How* are you going to make this event special over how you run your normal business? *How* are you going to put the odds in your favor?

- *Why* even have a sale or promotion in the first place? *Why* should your targeted customers even buy from you?

This list just gives a general example of how to use the six questions. You need to decide how to customize these questions as they relate to your own business. The more questions you can ask, based on the basic six words, the more answers you'll have and the more money you'll make. If you follow my suggestions and use this information, you should see better results than if you were to go after your target market with a less systematic approach.

Story Twelve

A few years ago, a wholesale company approached me to help improve their sales. They had done direct mail before, but their current results were falling flat. This company specialized mainly in the food business. They would first buy overstocked, overproduced, off-spec, and canceled orders from manufacturers all over the United States. They would then sell these products to their network of food and retail establishments, which in turn would sell to the general public at a reduced price. I was hired to stimulate the manufacturers to sell those items to my client.

In the beginning, I didn't know very much about my client's business. The first thing I did was to ask the six questions until I understood their business and how it worked. Two important aspects in the targeting of this campaign were identifying *who* and *what* were the right manufacturers for them to contact. When we agreed on the manufacturers, the next step was to determine *where* we would find them. We went to the S.I.C. (standard industry codes) which breaks down every business type into main categories and subcategories. As a rule I generally find a list that best suits my client's needs and have them pick whom to target. (After all, who should know better than the clients as to *who* and *why* people buy from them?) My client chose basic food manufacturers. From all the information that I had acquired, I now designed a mail piece that I felt would work.

A few days after we mailed the ad, the client's phone started to ring. From the phone calls came orders and new contacts. The campaign worked.

A few months later, my client called and wanted to do it again. He told me that he had received quite a few calls from grain and flour manufacturers which didn't help him. He said he wanted more frozen foods and ice cream. (I don't know why he didn't tell me this in the beginning; maybe I didn't ask enough questions.) I suggested using the food manufacturing subcategories so that we could pinpoint exactly what he wanted. On the next mailing, having identified the *"where"* more specifically, the advertising worked wonderfully again and much more to the customer's liking.

In many cases your first shot out of the box may hit the target but not the bull's-eye. The best approach is to do first what you think is right; then you can adjust your sights based on each attempt until you have the results you anticipated. Patience and knowledge coupled with feedback are key.

Sales

Do you pick out a territory or segment of the market and go after it. Or are you all over the place using the shotgun approach? Take some time and ask yourself the six questions as they relate to your sales career. (Don't use time when you would otherwise be working. Then you're just avoiding work, and we all know how salespeople love to do that).

These six questions are probably as old as the profession of selling itself. Answer the following sets of the six questions as they relate to what you need to know about selling to your present and future customers. (You might even learn something about yourself.)

WHO
- is your customer?
- is the contact?
- is using your product or service?
- is the decision-maker?

WHAT
- makes someone use or buy your product or service?
- makes you better than your competition?
- constitutes a good or bad prospect for you?
- makes a customer a good or bad customer?
- made you choose this profession in the first place?
- are you doing with the six questions?

WHEN

- do customers use your goods or services?
- is the best time to call on them?
- is their buying cycle?
- is the best time to close the deal or shut up?
- are you going to make or take the time to do this exercise?

WHERE

- is your territory?
- do they use your product or service?
- is their or your price point so they buy?
- is your best target?
- do you make the biggest bang for the buck?
- do you go to find more customers?

HOW

- do they buy?
- will you contact them?
- do they contact you?
- do you make the product easy for your customers to buy?
- do you present or demonstrate your product?
  (only amateurs say "pitch")
- do you track your progress or results?

WHY

- are you in sales?
- should they even want your product or service?
- are you selling this product or service?
- should they buy from you?
- should they buy now?
- should I do this exercise in the first place?
- are you reading this book?

Did you answer the questions? Or did you say to yourself *I'll do it later*? Chances are that if you took the time just now to do this little exercise, you care about your career. If you just skimmed over the questions thinking you'd return to them later, maybe you should reconsider whether or not you should even be in sales. Sales is a real profession, not a hobby. Sales is not something you do in your spare time if you want to be successful; sales is something you do *all* the time.

Doing in-home sales of Craftmatic was a sink-or-swim situation. Treading water was not an option. If I didn't make a sale, I didn't make a dime. Driving an hour or two each way to my appointments wasn't unusual. During that time I would listen to motivational or sales tapes and practice new closes and techniques. Ninety-five percent of my presentation from the moment I said "Hello: was rehearsed and scripted, but my customers never knew it. Do you really think you can improve or find your weak spots if you're always winging it? Tom Hopkins, who is one of the greatest salesman and sales trainers in the world, taught me that amateurs wing it. Professionals practice, drill and rehearse. Professionals never stop learning and honing their skills. Sales is a learned skill, and succeeding at it is exceedingly difficult. For that reason, these six questions are *critical* to your career.

Story Thirteen

I had driven over an hour to arrive at my Craftmatic appointment. In the Craftmatic sales process, the first thing you did after you gained rapport with the target was to ask a series of questions. The questions I devised were mainly based on the six questions we've been reviewing here. You needed to know what and who you were dealing with and whether or not your appointment was a viable candidate for the bed. After establishing that the person you were speaking to was a good prospect, the next thing you did was to show them a twenty-minute video.

The video showed all the models and sizes and how the bed worked. After the video was over, I would ask them, "So far, does this bed sound like it's going to give you what you're looking for?" If they said "yes," the next step was in the bedroom, where I could see what they were sleeping on now and discuss what they wanted. In the bedroom was also where we determined the size of Craftmatic that they wanted. Most people said they wanted the biggest and the best we had. Of course, they made that statement before they saw the price of that model. My mistake was taking their claim of biggest and best and believing it. I was told that the real sale was made in the bedroom (no, not *that* kind of sale), but up until this day that idea never really hit home with me.

After choosing the size they wanted, we then went back to their kitchen table to go over the options and prices. In the story I'm relating here, the people really wanted and could use the benefits of this bed. When they saw however, how much the best model cost, cold feet set in. Now keep in mind they didn't need the top-of-the-line bed which included features they didn't have to have. The next model down was the right bed for them, including all the features they truly required.

The difference was like a car that comes in two models— which are exactly the same except that one goes from zero-to-sixty in seven seconds and the top-of-the-line model makes it in five and a half seconds. If you blink, that's the difference, but the top-of-the-line car can cost as much as fifteen thousand dollars more for essentially the same car. How often do you really need to go that fast that quickly anyway? Ever?

That scenario is what I was dealing with here. I tried to sell them the bed they said they wanted, not what they needed. From that moment on, I could forget about them buying *any* bed, and they didn't. I blew it. Losing the sale was my fault, and I'll tell you why in a minute.

When I left that home, I was steaming mad—not at them, but at myself. One of my good characteristics is that instead of blaming someone else for what goes wrong, I try to use my anger to figure out how not to let a bad outcome happen again. That's one secret of how to become great at any endeavor. For this particular situation, I kept asking myself the six questions:

- *Who* could have helped me?
- *What* did I do wrong?
- *When* did I blow it?
- *Where* could I go for help?
- *How* can I make sure this particular situation never happens again?
- *Why* did I let it happen?

Some questions on this list frankly stumped me, so I called John Girty owner of the Craftmatic distributorship I represented and asked if he could help me with my problem. (Never be afraid to ask for help.) He asked me if I asked them the following question: "If the model you want is a little more than you are willing to spend, would the next size and model be okay?" Of course I said "no," and he said, "That's your answer. When you're selling Craftmatics, always have an agreed-on fallback position before you leave the bedroom, and never go to the next step until you do." I took his advice and that scenario never happened to me again.

Life

When we talk about your life targets, we're talking about your hopes and dreams. In order to realize your hopes and dreams, you need goals. How are you going to arrive at your target or destination unless you know where you're going? And will you know when you've made it there?

First we're talking here about your thoughts. Your thoughts are the fastest, most powerful energy on the planet. Your thoughts move at the speed of light, approximately 186,300 miles per second. That's seven and a half times around the world per second. What's more, nothing can stop your thoughts; they penetrate everything.

Now that you know how powerful your thoughts are (I suspect you already had a clue), what are you going to do with that power?

I hope you'll want to direct them in the right direction, for youself. Direct the six questions inward. How do these six questions relate to you as a human being? Have you ever asked yourself some of these questions? If not, now's the time.

WHO
- am I?
- do I believe in?
- can I count on?
- counts on me?
- do I love?
- loves me?
- do I dislike?
- do I admire?

WHAT
- am I?
- do I stand for?
- do I believe in?
- motivates me?
- am I afraid of?
- is life all about?
- am I doing here?
- do I do best?

- have I overcome?
- do I need to overcome?
- brings me joy?
- have I always wanted to do but I'm afraid to do?

WHEN

- am I going to take the time to ask myself these questions?
- am I going to sit down and really figure out what I want?
- do I make time for my family?
- do I make time for myself?
- am I going to do what I know I should do?
- am I going to do whatever it is I want to do?
- am I going on vacation?
- do I tell the people that I love, that I love them?
- is this guy going to quit asking me all these questions?
(Not yet)

WHERE

- have I been?
- is my life going?
- do I need to be?
- do I want to be?
- do I want to go?
- have I been all my life?
- is an aspirin?
(All these questions are giving me a headache.)

HOW

- is my life going?
- do I figure out what it is that I really want?
- do I express my feelings?
- am I going to get to where I want to be?
- do I know when to say no?
- do I learn to take risks?

- do I learn to ask for help?
- do I learn to stand up for myself?
- am I going to handle the answers to these questions?

WHY

- am I here?
- have I chosen the path I'm on?
- am I doing the things I'm doing?
- did I do the things that I've done?
- did I let myself get in this position?
- do I care what they think?
- do I let people do those things to me?
- is it never enough?
- am I reading this book?
- haven't I taken the time to do this before?
- am I driving through life with the brakes on?

Is your brain swollen yet? Most people have a hard time answering those questions and the way you answer them today is probably different than the way you answered them a year ago, and a year from now you'll probably answer them differently too. If you took the time to do this exercise I commend you. Not every question is for every person. If a question makes you really uncomfortable, then you have a good indicator that the question is important for you. The question wouldn't cause you discomfort unless it was hitting home.

These are not all the questions you should ask yourself. You need to ask yourself difficult questions every day if you want to grow as a human being. What are the questions that apply directly to you? Only you know what they are. The questions I've posed above are just the beginning of your quest. For real growth come up with your own.

What experiences has this chapter reminded you of? Write them down right here, right now before you go on to the next chapter.

Write down now: What is it that you can really zero in on to improve on your business, relationships or life right now as it relates to your answers to the six questions?

THE RECIPE:

NOW THAT WE'VE COME THIS FAR

UNDERSTAND...

EVERY INGREDIENT

IS

IMPORTANT

SOME MORE THAN OTHERS

LEAVE ONE OUT

AND

YOU MAY NOT LIKE
HOW IT TASTES

IF YOU'RE

NOT GETTING
THE

RESULTS

YOU WANT

MAYBE
IT'S THE

CHEF

Ever think about that?... Now let's continue

CHAPTER SIX

LESS IS MORE

THE MAIL

IS

BROAD

STA

PIECE

YOUR

CAST

TION

ARE YOU BROAD

W. I. I.

IF

REMEMBER SERGEANT

HEAR

This is not only *true* in Sales and Direct

CASTING THEIR

F. M.

NOT

CARTER'S, "I CAN'T

YOU!"

Mail, but <u>in</u> <u>every</u> other Advertising <u>medium</u>

YOU
HAVE
A
MAXIMUM
OF
7 SECONDS
TO
SATISFY
AND
NOURISH

THEIR

W. I. I. F. M.

<u>NOT</u>

YOUR

EGO

LESS

IS

MORE

FEED

THEM

<u>ONLY</u>

WHAT

COUNTS

Advertising and Direct Mail

Have you ever noticed that when you're in a conversation with someone and their mind is somewhere else, they can't hear you? Of course you have. Something like that happens to all of us every day. Isn't it frustrating? How would you feel if you were paying thousands of dollars for people to hear you and their minds were somewhere else? Isn't that what advertisers are doing to us every day?

Suppose you're one of those advertisers that no one is listening to. People are not listening to your advertisement because you didn't get their attention; you didn't attract them. Without their attention, they can't possibly tune into your message. Let me ask you a question. As an advertiser, would you be happy about that? I doubt it. Probably you're just the opposite. Here's the dilemma.

Every day we are bombarded with speed, sound, information, and images. We are overwhelmed with verbal and nonverbal communication. I think that in the early eighties and before, most people had the impression that they could keep up with the world around them. Not anymore! With the introduction of cable and satellite television, fax machines, cell phones, home computers, e-mail, and the World Wide Web, you can forget about keeping up. Staying on top of world events was challenging enough when we just had televisions with antennas, AM and FM radio, magazines, and the newspaper.

What does this all mean? We *have all gone into the information overload state.* Our brains can only handle so many impressions at a time and still function normally. In order to stay sane we automatically start becoming very selective as to who and what we let into our consciousness, especially when it comes to advertising of any kind. We are bombarded with it. Just look at the Sunday paper, your mailboxes both for letters and e-mail, and the stations now available on TV and radio. Did you know that a one-hour television show is really only about forty minutes long? In that hour, you're watching about twenty minutes of commercials!

Did you ever notice how they hook you in a two-hour movie? First they play twenty to twenty-five minutes straight with no interruptions. Then they ease in one or two quick commercials to keep you there. Then they start shortening the space between commercials and adding more of them. By the time you're in the second hour of the movie they are playing ten commercials every commercial break, and shortening the time between them until there's a commercial break every five minutes. How do I know this? I've kept track and counted them. Check this out for yourself sometime and you'll see that I'm right.

Why am I telling you all of this? Because if you plan on having any success at all with your advertising, regardless of the medium, you'll need to make sure that your target is receiving your message. But first, you have to know that the audience is letting the message in, given that most of the people you're trying to reach are experiencing information overload. So let's discuss how we enter your audience's brain. (Whoever said advertising wasn't brain surgery?)

First, you enter your target's brain by freezing it. No, I don't mean you have to bring everyone home with you and lay their heads in your icebox. What I mean by "freezing their brain" is temporarily stopping their thought patterns and putting their brains in neutral. How do you that? Simple. You slam their brains into reverse while their thoughts are going forward at 186,300 miles a second. *What?* I just did it to you. *Huh?* That's right! Let me explain.

Slamming someone's brain into reverse is *simple and easy to do*. Let's return to the original premises.

Everyone is busy and preoccupied with their lives.
People's brains are on overload.
Everyone's thoughts are racing at 186,300 miles per second.
Your target audience wants to know "what's in it for me."

And a new one . . .

You only have two to five with a maximum of seven seconds to get your message across, or it's over.

With those premises in mind, let's continue.

In order to *put their minds in neutral, we must first interrupt their thought patterns momentarily*. Why only momentarily? Because that's all you have. Within seconds, their brain returns to the hundreds of thoughts flowing in their minds.

You interrupt a person's thought patterns—throw it in reverse—by saying or doing something that makes them say either out loud or to themselves, "*What?*" or "*Huh?*" *Their brain is now in neutral*, which means that it's temporarily open for receiving.

For example, if we were having a conversation and right in the middle of our conversation you said to me with no warning, "Your ears look green," I would probably say, "What?" or "Huh?" Then you'd have me in neutral. Experiment: Try saying or doing weird, out-of-the-ordinary things to people and watch their brains freeze.

How do you freeze their brains with direct mail? First, prompting them to open your envelope and second, having a headline that interrupts their thought pattern. You need not insult them or say something vulgar. You want their minds to be open, not mad or defensive. Once their minds are open, you have your two to five seconds—with an absolute maximum of seven seconds—to get your message across.

We have a product called *Stealth-Mail*™ that does exactly that: it sneaks into their minds undetected and temporarily short-circuits their brain so that we can get our message across..

Now that we're in their minds, let's talk about the message. As I mentioned at the beginning of this chapter, "Less is more," which in advertising and direct mail translates into "Feed them only what counts."

What counts? Only their W.I.I.F.M.: *What's in it for me?* With that premise in mind, create your ads with as few words and pictures as possible. Convey your message with some questions unanswered. Make your audience take the next step. What is the next step?

The next step is the response you want out of your ad. Perhaps it's a phone call, mailing in a return postcard, ordering a catalog, going to your Web site, or coming in to your place of business. The ultimate final step is spending their money with you.

That step may not be the end of the transaction but merely the beginning. Each step they take along the way to spending money with you can create mini- or maxi-gratifications. You want them to feel good about what they are doing. If you want your advertising to really work, make sure that the steps they have to take are also simple and easy. That's where a planned sales process fits in (see last chapter) Remember, *less is more.*

How many of you have ever painted a door, window, wall, room, or anything else in your house? Probably most of you

THE 100 MILLION DOLLAR PLAYBOOK

have. Let me ask you a question: How many strokes does it take to paint a doorframe? Chances are most of you have no idea and think that the question itself is strange. When I was in my prime as a painter, I would paint a doorframe in twenty-seven strokes. Not twenty-six, not twenty-eight. Twenty-seven, period. How do I know this and why am I so precise? Because, less is more. Let me explain.

Story Fourteen

I was eighteen years old and in my last year of high school. My friend Nick and I decided to start our own painting company. Keep in mind that we really had no idea what we were doing, but we weren't going to let a little thing like that stop us. We formed a company called Blossom Decorating. (As of this writing, the company still exists and Nick still owns it.) I can't tell you how many times a customer would ask us if we knew how to do a particular thing and we'd always say yes. In the beginning, most of the time we had no idea of how to do what we said we knew how to do. Learning sometimes was a nightmare, but we would find out how to do what we already said we could, and then do it. Somehow or another we would almost always make it turn out good. Nick and I always wanted to be the best, and the lack of knowledge in any particular area wasn't going to stop us. Because of our ignorance coupled with a need and desire to learn, over time we became really good painters, not to mention paperhangers!

After a couple of years I went out on my own and started a company called Northfield Decorating. A few years later I was helping Nick on a big job. He had this guy named Joe G. who was the fastest paperhanger I had ever seen. He could also paint like lightning and did it perfectly. One day I asked Joe, "How do you paint so fast?" He gave me a secret that I use in my life to this day. He received this secret from an old-time painter. The secret was *"Never waste a stroke and make every stroke count."* That comment was one of my biggest lessons on the premise that less is more. I took his advice and over time I figured out how to paint almost anything in the best way with the least amount of strokes possible. (Now you understand why a doorframe takes twenty-seven strokes. (Want to know the twenty-seven-stroke method? Come to my Web site, *www.100Milliondollar.com*, and I'll give it to you.)

Story Fifteen

To give you an example of how powerful the Less-Is-More premise is, I'm going to share another experience with you. I was painting an apartment complex job with five other painters. The complex had dozens of buildings and each building had eleven back doors with windows. On average, each painter would take one hour to paint one door including the windows. One day I had to leave the job early, so the next day I needed to make up my work from the previous day. When I came in the next morning I started right away and painted eleven doors in sixty-six minutes. Not only did I finish in lightning speed, but they were all perfect. For each door, that's six minutes rather than one hour.

When I told the other painters I was done, they said, "Well, that leaves you ten more doors to do."

I said, "You don't understand. I'm done for the day. I finished all eleven doors."

Needless to say they didn't believe me and came down from their ladders to go over to the building I was working on to see for themselves. They were blown away. They asked how the heck I did that and I said, "Never waste a stroke and make every stroke count."

An interesting thing happens when you try and figure out how to do something the best way possible with the least amount of steps. Great ideas and techniques come to you that help you accomplish your goals.

Sales

How much time are you wasting in your sales career. Time that you could be selling and closing? How much time do you spend studying your craft? Do you have your presentation down to a science? Are you talking more than listening? Are you running around in circles?

Do you still believe those same old excuses as the truth? How about the classic "Send me some information"? How many of those prospects did you ever sell? Not many I'm sure.

In the world of sales, I'm afraid that most salespeople have the mantra backwards. They think that more is less. You know what I'm talking about: the sweaty, glad-handed, pushy have-I-got-a-deal-for-you-today, except the approach is usually more subtle than that. More like a nice, friendly, talk-your-ear-off professional visitor.

Do you have a specific goal in mind for every step of your sales process? Do you even have specific steps and segments to your sales process? *Do you even have a sales process?* Or do you just wing it and whatever happens, happens? Do you take your sales process and make it have as few words and steps as possible? Have you worked and reworked each and every step until each step gives you the desired results?

Do you want to know how to do that? You don't want me to tell you now, do you? Right here? In this book?

What do you think I have been doing? I just did it to you again. *Right! I've been asking, not telling.* By asking questions, you say less and get more. More *what*? More information. Remember, information is power! How are you going to sell something to someone if you don't know who or what you're dealing with? Remember the last chapter on the six questions? You'll be able to get more of whatever you want or need to accomplish by mostly asking, not telling.

One of the ways you ask instead of tell is to rephrase what you're saying into questions instead of statements. Here's an example of telling: "We have a new widget that slices, dices, and saves you time and your money. Do you want to buy one?" *YUK!* Unfortunately most salespeople have an approach that basically sounds like that form of telling.

Instead of telling, what if you said, "Do you mind if I ask you a few questions?" Always wait for them to say okay before you go ahead. "Do you ever need to slice or dice things? Would you say your time is important to you? I don't suppose you'd be interested in a product that could do all of those things and save you money too?" If they ask "What is it" or "What have you got," then you tell them, but don't tell them until they ask you to.

What if they say, "No, I wouldn't be interested"? That's great for you, because you can go on to someone else who is interested without wasting your time and effort.

Unfortunately, this one chapter doesn't allow us enough time and space to explain all the how's and why's of the need to ask more than tell. Some terrific sales books are available that go into greater detail on this subject. I would suggest that you read *"Can I Have 5 Minutes of Your Time"* by Hal Becker, *"Mastering the Art of Selling"* by Tom Hopkins, *"Secrets of Closing the Sale"* by Zig Ziglar, and *"You Can't Teach a Kid To*

Ride a Bicycle at a Seminar", by David Sandler. A good audiotape set on the subject is *"Psychology of Selling: The Art of Closing Sales"*, by Brian Tracy.

Story Sixteen

Back when I first started in the direct mail business I was knocking on doors. I knew of one dealership in town that did more direct mail than anyone else. Of course, I wanted that account. I had heard some derogatory rumors about the owner of this dealership—that he was arrogant and tough to work with—so I decided to go in there and find out for myself. (All those rumors were totally untrue; he was one of the nicest people I had ever met. Remember the chapter on "open the envelope or else"?)

I walked in and asked for the owner by name. (There's another hint: always have a name to ask for instead of just asking for the owner or manager of an establishment or company. Otherwise, they'll know you're a salesperson.) When Donn came out, I introduced myself and said, "Hi, my name is David Alan, and we do direct mail. I don't know, do you guys ever do stuff like that?" (Remember, I already knew they mailed like crazy, but I wanted to ask instead of tell.)

He said to me, "Sometimes, but we've run out of hooks." (A hook is a term used to describe a reason to come in or buy.) The average amateur salesperson at that point would have probably said, "Oh, have I got a hook for you!" and Donn would have probably said "No, thanks." Instead, as a pro, I continued asking instead of telling.

I said, "Oh, then you probably wouldn't be interested in any new hooks?"

He said, "Yes, I would, but I don't have any time to talk about it now."

I replied, "Neither do I. I was just driving by and thought I'd stop in."

So he said, "Come on into my office and let's set up a time to get together." That no-time-for-either-of-us turned into an hour and a half of laughing and talking. *We never even talked about direct mail.*

At the end of meeting, Donn said to me, "David, I'm not sure exactly what you do, but based on just being with you I'm sure it's good. We'll do business."

A few weeks later we had our first sale, and it was a great success. By 2 P.M. we had sold so many cars that Donn said, "Let's book some more sales right now," and we did! This account turned out to be one of the best I've ever had. We became great friends. As a matter of fact, he was even one of the groomsmen in my wedding!

A few years ago Donn sold his business, and he is still one of my closest and dearest friends. None of this would have been possible if I hadn't use the premises of *Less Is More* and *Open the Envelope.*

Life

Is your life so jumbled up that you can't even see straight? Do you not have enough hours in the day to do everything you need to do? Is everything in such disarray that you can never find what you're looking for? Do you open your closet full of clothes and can find nothing to wear? Is there too much month left at the end of the money? Do you never have enough time to spend with the people you love? Do any of these concepts sound familiar?

Welcome to the busy, cluttered, zillions-of-impressions world of the twenty-first century. How do you bring your crazy life under control?

"Less is more" should be your mantra if you want to get your life together. "What about money" you're thinking. Well, there's always an exception to the rule, but the more money you have, the more responsibility you have to use it correctly— if you want to be a worthwhile human being.

How does "less is more" apply to your life? Let's start with food. I don't know the exact figure but I'm safe in saying most of the U.S. population is overweight. Whether five or fifty pounds overweight, too much is too much. We only really need a handful of food at a sitting, not a bag full. When you eat less and properly, you gain the most important thing in your life: your health! By eating less you feel better, you look better, your clothes fit, and you have more energy. If you've ever experienced those things you know how great it feels. To quote a good friend of mine, Joe Garrett, "If you want to feel good, pass on the second trip to the salad bar".

Let's discuss clothes. Most people have more clothes than we really need. You probably have lots of items that you don't use or wear anymore. Give them away. Make room for the life you want now.

Ever go on vacation and realize how little we really need to be happy? Again I recommend a fantastic book on this subject called *Clear Your Clutter with Feng Shui* by Karen Kingston.

If you're like me you won't be able to put it down, because it's a really enjoyable, enlightening read.

How about your relationships? Are they quantity or quality? You may have a lot of acquaintances, but how many real friends—if any—do you really have? If you're not sure, just wait until something devastatingly traumatic happens in your life. You'll be shocked and amazed at how many people you thought were your friends scatter like a shotgun blast. If you have one friend left at a time like that, consider yourself blessed.

When my wife was growing up her father would tell her, "If you have one best friend in your life, you're lucky."

My wife would respond, "I have lots of friends."

He would say, "You'll see."

A bomb went off in my wife's life a few years ago. Guess how many of her lifelong friends went to her aid? You guessed it: none! Unfortunately her father was right. That's why I say again, "Less is More."

Go for the quality of life, not the quantity. Do you want to get a handle on your life? Start with your hopes and dreams, then transfer those hopes and dreams into major goals, your major goals into mini-goals, and your mini-goals into daily or weekly tasks. How do you eat a giant salami? One slice at a time.

Lots of books and courses on goal setting are available. I recommend Franklin Covey. Not only do they have all kinds of life planners, but also they have great courses that show you how to utilize these tools. Anyone can write down an appointment, but is that appointment moving you closer to or farther away from your goals? Franklin Covey's tools can show you how and why, *because without the why's, your life is just a trip, not a journey.*

What experiences has this chapter reminded you of? Write them down right here, right now, before you go on to the next chapter.

Write down now: What can I do to apply the premise of less is more in my business relationships, or life right now?

CHAPTER SEVEN

URGENCY CREATES ENERGY

URGENCY

CREATES

ENERGY

ENERGY

CREATES

ACTION

If you

CURR

$ $

You must

URGE

want

ENCY

$ $

create

NCY!

Advertising and Direct Mail

Let's just do a quick review of what we've covered so far in the book: the envelope or packaging, reasons for a sale, the best time for a sale, your target with the six questions, and less is more. Now the time has come to talk about urgency. Urgency is the igniter of your sale. If we give people an open window of when to come, they probably won't come. When I looked up the word *urgent* in the dictionary I gleaned the following: compelling immediate action, imperativeness, demanding immediate attention. In other words, *do it now or forget it!* Miss this and it's over! The early bird gets the worm, and you get zilch if you don't come! Urgency *gets people off their backsides.* If you don't set a deadline, whatever you want to do won't get done. Think about that.

Can you imagine throwing a party with no definite day or time? How many people do you think would show up? Not many, if any, I can assure you. How do you react when you have somewhere to go? Probably the closer the deadline, the more urgent you become as it relates to going there. Want to take the pressure off? Don't put a time limit on something important, but on the other hand, if you don't put a time limit on something important you'll probably have to settle for mediocrity.

A body in motion stays in motion, and a body at rest stays at rest. That premise underlies this chapter. If you want someone to get off the dime, you have to throw him or her a quarter. Making someone or something move is hard if that person or thing is stationary. That's why a body at rest stays at rest, unless you get that body to move.

How do you convince someone to move? You inject a stimulus into his or her world. The stimulus can be negative or positive, just as long as it serves its function. I know you've heard, "For every action, there's an equal and opposite reaction." The idea is to make people react first, then you move them with stimulation in the direction you want them to go. If you don't inspire them to move first, whatever you wanted from them is over before it starts.

The stimulant we're talking about in this chapter is urgency. That's because urgency is one of the strongest stimulants for a human being. Urgent means "Move, now!". It means "Time's almost up, and you'll miss out if you don't move." Urgency triggers another strong emotional response: fear of loss, which is greater than the desire for gain.

The easiest way to put the following concept is to do it honestly: *You need to exploit and recognize human nature if you want to bend it to your hopes and dreams.* Almost anything you want out of life must come through someone else, either directly or indirectly. This statement doesn't mean however, that you have to take advantage of people to their detriment. On the contrary, make sure that you're always offering someone a win-win situation. Give more service than people pay for or expect, and you'll be rewarded tenfold.

Time is the essence of urgency. When you squeeze time, urgency expands. The less time you have, the more urgency you create Urgency creates energy, and energy is the gas for your sale. Think of the following analogy: Imagine that your company's sale is a car. In order for your car to run, first you need to start it. Urgency is you starting the car—the igniter. In order for your car to run you need gas, the energy. Making the car to go where you want is the same as making your sale work. If your sale works, you are creating results (currency) from the urgency and energy. Your sale was a success, and you feel great about yourself. Who wouldn't want that?

One of the great things about urgency is that it creates massive energy. When a lot of people show up in the same tight timeframe and start buying things, we call that a *feeding frenzy.* The more people that are buying, the more people buy. Sales works like a chain reaction in that respect. This scenario is also known as "putting people under the ether." When you throw a big sale, you try and create that type of atmosphere.

Imagine going to a popular new restaurant. Sometimes you see a new restaurant that is so crowded that you assume it must be great because of all the people. On the other hand, haven't you also gone to a new restaurant at lunch or dinner and no one was there? You probably said, "Let's not go here. Something must be wrong with this place," whether or not there really was.

Urgency creates energy and excitement, two key ingredients in any successful sale. Use them both correctly, and you're bound to make more currency.

Story Seventeen, Part 1

I was doing a sale for this big Chevy store for the first time. They had about twenty salespeople. We were running a five-hour sale two days in a row. We took twenty thousand pieces and mailed ten thousand for Saturday's sale and ten thousand for Sunday's. Each sale of ten thousand pieces was for five hours only. These sales were what I call a "non- mooch" sale. In other words, gift seekers who came in for their free umbrella or steak knife set and had no intention of buying anything were eliminated up front. The only reason someone would come to this sale was if they wanted a new or newer vehicle. The average return on a non-mooch sale is an 0.25 to 0.5 percent response. These two sales gleaned a 1 percent return each day. We had one hundred people each day that wanted to buy cars in a five-hour period. The urgency of the mailer worked great!

Unfortunately, a downside exists to everything, and urgency is no different. A few attributes of urgency can backfire on you. They are as follows:

1. Not giving yourself enough time to prepare, which causes holes in your net. How are you going to catch anything if everything slips through your grasp?

2. Putting more on your plate than you could possibly eat. In other words, don't have a sale in a time frame if it's going to be impossible to take care of everyone who shows up.

Story Seventeen, Part 2: With only twenty salespeople and one hundred customers in five hours, serving everyone became an impossible task. We did great, but we lost about thirty people each day because we couldn't serve them all. That Monday, the dealership called those sixty people back and apologized. They even offered them more of a discount if they came back in, but most of them declined. The moral of this part of the story: after that experience, we gave people two days to come into that dealership instead of one, and we were able to take care of almost everyone.

Don't be afraid of experimentation or trying something new. The idea is to take what worked and continue that part. Then take what didn't work, if anything, and try something new based on what you have experienced from the experiments. Thomas Edison needed ten thousand experiments until he finally made the incandescent light. People would laugh and make jokes about him and his invention. When he was asked how could he fail at something ten thousand times and keep going, his retort was, "I haven't failed ten thousand times. I've learned ten thousand ways it doesn't work." With that knowledge and determination, he was able to light up the world!

Sales

Regarding urgency and sales, I'm going to address these topics from a different angle. When I was selling aluminum siding and new windows, the owner of the company told me a little story. (Yes, I was a tin man for a little while. Also, the movie "*Tin Man*" is a must for anyone in sales.)

Remember the old water pumps that you had to hand pump in order to pull up the water? They weren't like the faucets of today. Today we take for granted that you go to a faucet, turn on the water, and out it comes. Back in the days of hand pumps, you had to pump and pump before the water would start to come out. Once it did come out, you had to keep pumping for as long as you wanted the water to flow.

Let's say it takes twenty-five pumps before the water begins to come out. Now once it's flowing, every pump you pump gives water. What do you think would happen if you came back the next day and walked up to that pump and pumped it just once? Right, nothing. You would have to pump it twenty-four more times before you could get a drop. What does that have to do with urgency in closing a sale? Everything! Let me explain.

The average sales process goes through a sequence of events. Those events are the greeting, building rapport, asking questions, getting a commitment, presentation, closing the order, and the post-close. These sequence or set of steps may not be yours exactly, but I'm confident you understand the concept.

Could you imagine going through that entire process, except that when they wanted to place an order you said you'd come back next Thursday and do it then? What do you think would happen next Thursday when you came back, especially if you didn't review the previous week's presentation first to bring them back to where you were when you left? You probably wouldn't make the sale. Now I'm not talking about a sales process that normally take six months to complete. However, if you're involved in a process that does take six months and you're at eight months with no sale, maybe something is wrong. That something wrong is probably you. You have to give them a reason to buy now! In that challenge are the seeds of urgency.

How many of your "think-it-over"s or "maybe-we'll-order-next-time"s do you ever sell? Probably a minuscule amount, if any. If you've reached the decision makers and they are at the point of making a decision and they don't decide, you've lost. Remember, as my good friend, Joseph W. Schervish, taught me, "*Anything but yes is no.*" Think about that. I have and he's right.

You need to give people a reason to buy now instead of next week or next year. If you don't have a reason for your potential clients to buy now, create one. Make sure the reason you give them makes sense and nourishes their W.I.I.F.M. Maybe the urgency comes from saving money or receiving more of what you sell than they could for the same money if they waited. Depending on what you sell, maybe the urgency could pay off to them with a trip or a weekend getaway. The point is that urgency creates energy (a fire under their backside), energy creates action (making a decision now), and action creates currency (their action was ideally a "yes," and you're making more money). Even if their answer was "no," you now know where you stand with them and you can go on to the next one. *Remember: all you have is your valuable time. Don't let people waste it.*

Story Eighteen

When I was selling the Contour chair in the home, we had an advantage that almost no other product has. We were the only company in the world making that type of chair. Back when the first Mercury space program rockets were being developed, NASA came to Contour for help on the rocket seats. Contour had the only chairs in the world that were anatomically correct to fit the contours of a person's body, thus providing total body support. We had a unique, fantastic product.

Almost everyone who saw the presentation we gave wanted the chair. The only challenge we really had was the price. The Contour chair was expensive. Back in the late 1980's, my average chair sale was around three thousand dollars. Most of the chairs were custom-made. Not only did the customer pick out their materials but they also chose the chair base, arm style, heat and massage. The kicker was that we took numerous body measurements of the customer so that the chair would be made to fit that exact body.

I use to drive up in a customer's driveway with my Mercedes, step out wearing a beautiful suit, and go to the door. I knew they were watching me from the window. When I would come inside, they would almost always say to me, "Boy, business must be good." I would always say that business is great. They would say, "Those chairs must be expensive," and I would respond, "They sure are."

In part of my introduction and questioning period, I would let them know that we only come out once; we don't come back, and if you want a chair you have to buy it from me today or you can't have one. (Remember we had to measure them for the chair.) I used to love that advantage. No stores carried the Contour chair. I wasn't arrogant when I explained the conditions, I was just being honest. I would also say that

I had some great specials today that the customer could take advantage of because we don't come back. (That offer of the specials coupled with the fact we didn't come back were the reason to buy today, the urgency.)

I didn't sell everyone I made a presentation to, but I did very well. During my time selling the Contour chair I must have done over one thousand presentations. Not one of those presentations who didn't buy, but said "we'll think about it" or "we have to check on something and we'll call you back tomorrow with an order" ever did. Not a single one! *Remember to create urgency, because anything but yes is no.*

Life

Are you a couch potato with a microwave mindset?™ (you want everything now, but don't want to work for it.)

How long do you have to live? Do you really know? Most of us don't. I think that's a blessing. Who would want that hanging over their head? But what if you knew you only had one week to live. Do you think you would squander it watching TV and sleeping till noon? Or do you think you'd be up at the crack of dawn so you could get as much out of every day as possible. I think most of us wouldn't want to waste a minute.

How long do you really think you have to live? Again, your answer is probably "I don't know," because most of us really have no idea when we're going to check out. What would be wrong with living each day as if it really was your last? We've all heard that statement before. Most of us think, though, that we're going to be here forever. Now, you certainly have to understand how ludicrous that way of thinking really is.

What kind of life do you think you would experience if you really put everything you could into each and every day? Stop reading for a few minutes, close your eyes, and just imagine. Go on, I'll still be here when you come back.

* * *

Well, what happened? Did you do it? If you did, you probably saw and felt some wonderful things. *Most of what you imagined is possible if you put urgency into your life and go after what you want like there's no tomorrow.* Who knows, maybe for you there won't be a tomorrow. But whether or not there is, your life is the experience you were born to experience. Try living life every day as if it's your last. Do as much as you possibly can. Do it for one day. Then try another. If you like how that feels, do another. Now you're on a roll, keep going. *If you take this one piece of advice and use it, you'll be the happiest you've ever been. I can't think of anything better than that! Can you?*

What experiences has this chapter reminded you of? Write them down right here, right now before you go on to the next chapter.

Write down now: How can I use my experiences coupled with this new knowledge of using urgency to improve on my business, relationship or life right now?

CHAPTER EIGHT

SOWING MAKES YOU SOAR

SOWING

MAKES

YOU

SOAR

EVERYDAY

IS

PLANTING

DAY

ONLY

SPECIAL
DAYS

ARE...

RESERVED

FOR

HARVESTING

SOME SEEDS

GROW

QUICKLY

WHILE OTHERS

<u>TAKE</u> <u>TIME</u>

TO

MATURE

WHICH LEADS US TO...

Just because now is the microwave generation doesn't mean that people and things can just come to you at the push of a button. Sure you can order off the Internet and call for a pizza, but you're paying for those things. If you want people, a relationship, more businesses, or anything else that can't be bought, you have to have patience.

Sowing makes you soar, and sowing can make you sore. Did I say this process was easy? *Sowing* means to spread or scatter seeds in hopes that they'll grow. In my use here, sowing means planting an overabundant amount of deeds, thoughts, words, and ideas.

What do you think would happen if you planted a garden and every morning you dug up all your seeds to see if they've grown? Right, nothing. Let's try another one. What if I gave you a cup of grass seed and had you spread those seeds over a small area? Do you think every single seed would take root and grow? Of course not. So why do you think that every act or task you make must have an instant result and gratify you immediately? But most of you do, you might tell me otherwise if we were face-to-face, but so many people really feel this way.

If you're an advertiser, you expect almost every person who hears or sees your advertisement to care about or want your goods and services. Sorry, most of them —I repeat *most of them* —don't want what you're offering to them. At least not now, but maybe later. (We saw in the last chapter where "later" often leads: nowhere.)

Remember the story about the guy who came into my locksmith store five years after I handed him a card? What if I had said to that gentleman when he took my card, "Sir, if you don't want my locksmithing services right this second, you can't have my card"? Sounds crazy, but that's how many people think. You don't think so? Are you telling me that you don't want to make every sale or land every job? Or that if you don't get the things you want, that you don't get bummed out? Are you saying that if you are or were single and you wanted to make a date with someone you liked, that you weren't scared that they would say no? If you didn't care, you wouldn't have wanted to ask the person out in the first place.

Nothing in life is guaranteed except living and dying. In life, like gardening, you must plant much more than you expect to harvest, and you must not take it personally and have it demotivate you when one or even a lot of your seeds take time or don't even grow at all.

Sometimes you're going to have complete gardens that no longer bloom or huge mature trees that all of a sudden don't bear fruit anymore. *Sometimes in life your sources and avenues are going to dry up on you, and you're going to have to plant a new garden.* Maybe a client doesn't use you anymore; maybe a relationship has gone sour or someone has died. Massive change happens, and then you have to pick yourself up and go plant a whole new garden of and for your life. (As I was writing this chapter, the World Trade Center and the Pentagon were attacked. You want to talk about massive change right now? From where you're sitting, you know all the changes that have resulted from these events.)

The message of this chapter is to *keep planting.* Don't depend on what's already coming in. Don't give too much power to any one person, place, or thing. Everything you try, may not bring you the desired results. You need to keep planting, reap when you can, and keep planting. The more you plant, the more that grows. The more that grows, the stronger you get.

Do you know how bamboo grows? For most species of bamboo, very little growth occurs for the first one or two years, but during that time the plant is actually putting down a deep, complex root system. Once the growth that you can't see has been accomplished, bamboo grows outward and upward with incredible zeal. Some species have been clocked at growing as much as four feet in a twenty-four-hour period.

Just think of the possibilities you have and what magnificent things you can achieve if you have and use your determination and patience.

Life, business, and projects have their seasons just like nature.

Spring is the time to plant for new growth; The time to start something new—like fresh new ideas, opportunities, friendships, or romance. As far as the seasons of life are concerned, spring is also the time of your birth.

Summer is the time for growth and peaking—expansion, growing pains, and great lessons learned.

Fall is for harvesting, enjoying the fruits of your labor, regardless of what kind of fruits they are. Fall can also be the time for massive change, the shedding of old skin, friends, situations, and feelings.

Winter is practically dormant; in a life span, winter is the time of death. Winter can also be when you're in a rut, stagnant, or not growing, or turning cold in your heart and on the world. Winter is also a time of rest, a time to hibernate or to recharge your batteries.

Pay attention to the seasons in your life, if you do, you will reap the benefits of seeing clearly many things that are not easy to comprehend.

What have you previously done in your life or career that you have had to plant and nurture for a long time? Then after an extended period of time you received massive growth or abundance from it. (Think of a hobby, sport, relationship, job, money, success, or love.) Write it down now!

Now use your experiences of success and this new information or inspiration to spur you on to bigger, better, and greater things in your life. Write those things down right now. Remember, as the motivational speaker Les Brown says, "It's possible!"

CHAPTER NINE

THE MARKET, THAT MOMENT

TM

THE MARKET

THAT MOMENT

TM

DID YOU KNOW

IT'S NOT

CHRISTMAS EVERY DAY?

EVERY DAY IS DIFFERENT,

WHEN YOU GET

THAT SPECTACULAR SALE,

BE THANKFUL

BECAUSE,

EVERY SALE IS DIFFERENT

IT BOILS DOWN TO . . .

TM TM

THE MARKET
THAT MOMENT

THAT'S THE WAY IT IS

AND

THAT'S HOW IT'S

ALWAYS

GOING TO BE

IT'S LIKE GRAVITY

YOU CAN'T CHANGE IT

LEARN TO WORK

WITH IT

FIND THE TIMES THAT

IT'S GOING YOUR WAY

AND

CAPITALIZE

ON THEM

Direct Mail

I received a phone call the other day from one of my clients who was calling to tell me how his sale went. He said that "We crushed," which to him meant that the results were phenomenal. Great news, right? Yes and no.

When you do a direct mail piece or any other type of sale to spur on a great deal of business, it's great when that business comes in but it also sets a precedent that is hard to repeat. I have helped numerous companies set sales records with my direct mail. Yet some companies become spoiled, and an otherwise decent sale becomes a dud or "just okay" in their minds, which is not how you should look at your results. Let me give you an example.

Story Nineteen

A finance manager from a car dealership called me to ask if I could do a sale for him. I had been doing nine sales a month for this particular dealership for a long time. The previous general manager there had asked me to come up with a special type of sale for them. The success they had experienced with my direct mail was strong and steady. Over a period of time, we had doubled the dealership's amount of business. The only reason they stopped doing business with me was because of a management change, and this new manager wasn't big on direct mail. He had his own ideas of how to advertise, and everyone is welcome to their opinion. Unfortunately for them, in a few months his method of newspaper advertising resulted in a drop in their sales back to where they were before we were hired. He then tried a bunch of other direct mail companies, but still to no avail.

With a lot of prodding from the finance manager and salespeople continually asking for my unique direct mail sales approach, the new manager decided to try one. The sale went great, and they sold twenty-five cars off of a five-thousand-piece mailer. (Keep in mind that approximately three car sales were needed to pay for my direct mail sale; after that every car sale was profit.) In the 1980s and early to mid-1990s, twenty-five cars sold would have been a good sale, but not unbelievable. But in the year 2000 this was a great sale, like selling fifty cars in previous years. Of course, the dealership reordered. The next sale sold twelve cars—still a good sale and better than average. Guess what happened next? Right, they quit because they got spoiled on the one sale of twenty-five cars instead of looking at the big picture that combining the sales results together they mailed ten thousand pieces and sold a total of thirty-seven cars.

In order for you to really get the picture of what I'm saying let me explain how this works. The average profit on a car sale in the year 2001 is approximately $1,600. That figures includes profit off the car sale itself, finance commission, extended warranty etc. My average direct mail sale for five thousand pieces is $5,000. Now let's do the math.

Cost to customer: Two direct mail sales @ $5,000 each = $10,000
Results: Thirty-seven car sales @ $1,600 each = $59,200
Profit = $59,200 sales minus $10,000 expense = $49,200.

I don't know about you, but anytime I can invest $10,000 to make $49,200 in two weekends, I'm in. How about you? I would hope you're in, too. But this particular car dealership apparently thought that almost 500 percent profit in two weeks wasn't enough.

My smart dealers know that every sale is not going to be a record breaker. They also know that by staying in the direct mail game, the results will typically average out to be a profitable win, and isn't that why companies advertise in the first place?

What I'm trying to convey here is that not every day is Christmas. *But what's wrong with the weekend?* Isn't that what most people look forward to anyway? When it's over, people can't wait until the next one. Why not have that same philosophy when it comes to having a sale or enjoying something in your life? *Both life and business are a series of peaks and valleys,* and *there's no silver bullet.* Be realistic and look at the big picture or the long haul. Otherwise you'll never be satisfied . . . with anything. Don't let Christmas make you greedy. *Be thankful for what you've got and what you get.*

Sales

If you are in sales, you know that sometimes it seems like you could sell ice to Eskimos. Then at other times, you can't give away a life raft to a drowning man. My advice to you is to always keep going through the good times and the bad. When you hit those times when you're unstoppable, double your efforts and take advantage of being on a roll. As sure as you came up, you'll come down. Make sure that you've built yourself a sufficient money cushion so that you can keep your good attitude through the tough times. Keep plugging; sure enough you'll come back on top.

Life

Life is a pendulum. At some times we feel strong, and other times we feel weak. When you feel strong, almost everything goes your way. You feel good, you're happy and confident, and most things roll off your back with ease. Your relationships, health, business, and hobbies are all peaking. Physics, though, says what goes up must come down, even though sometimes we think we're immune to that law. Why do we think that way? Because we're human and sometimes we think because of our God-given reason, nature doesn't apply to us.

Then comes the rude awakening. Life slaps us upside the head and maybe even drops us in the toilet. Sound familiar? If you've been on this planet for any length of time, you've had this experience. Nothing goes right, people are mad at you, you feel like garbage and a failure, and that's just from the first fifteen minutes after waking up.

So what's a person to do? Realize that the pendulum is just swinging you to the negative side, and that in time the pendulum will swing you back. Remember: especially in your down times, it's not what happens to you. *It's how you deal with what happens to you.* Just realize that all life is cyclical, and your own life is no different. Find something that you like to do that gives you joy and go do it. Realize that your life *will* cycle back to the positive. You don't think so? Just watch the changes in the seasons or the change of the moon. *They always come back around, and so will you.*

Write down when you have had terrible things happen to you in your life and you were at the bottom.

Now write how you came out of these negative experiences.

Write what you learned from your experience, how it contributes to who and what you are now. Write down the good and write down the bad.

Finally write down how can you use this experience or information to help you in your life now and going forward.

CHAPTER TEN

THE POST OFFICE IS YOUR FRIEND

THE

POST OFFICE

IS YOUR

FRIEND

and/or

PARTNER

AN

INTRICATE PART

OF YOUR

SUCCESS

TREAT THEM LIKE

YOUR ALLY

NOT YOUR

ADVERSARY

Let's face it,

They're not perfect

But then again

Who or what is?

Create a

Relationship

With your

Main Post Office

They're there to

Help You

Take advantage of it

Postage

First Class

or

Standard

Which one's the best?

First class is always better when time is of the essence.

However

Standard saves you

Lots of $$$

when you're not in a rush

PRE-SORT

REPORTS

ARE

WORTH

THEIR

WEIGHT

IN

GOLD

Not only do

They speed up

Your mail delivery

They can qualify you for

BIG

$$$

Savings

The message about the post office is the same message I recommend in treating any other vendor or person. That message is *to be nice to everyone and to treat people like you would like to be treated.* It's that simple.

CHAPTER ELEVEN

SMARTER NOT HARDER

SMARTER

NOT

HARDER

MOTION

ALONE

IS NOT

ACCOMPLISHMENT

Here are the questions everyone wants answered: How can I get more for less without sacrificing quality or people, and how can I do a better job at anything by working *smarter rather than harder*. People can be foolish in trying to save a nickel but they end up losing a dollar in the process. Think of the car dealer who thought that almost 500 percent profit in fourteen days wasn't an appropriate investment.

Another side of the same coin, so to speak, is what's wrong with spending 80 cents instead of a dollar for the exact same thing? Or what's wrong with figuring out how to do a job or task with less movements? That's what I did when I painted a doorframe in twenty-seven strokes.

Maybe this issue hits you in terms of buying in bulk or larger quantities to save money or doing a task better so that it costs less or lasts longer.

Look at what you do and see if you can accomplish it better, faster, stronger, or cheaper. Keeping this quest in mind, remember the old saying, "Don't be penny wise and pound foolish."

In all the purchases I've made in my life, I have never been sorry for buying the best of anything. Have you? But I think we've all experienced regret at not buying something better.

Sales

In sales, how do you reach more customers or bigger customers using less time or effort? Remember that all you have is your time. How do you make it more productive or profitable? Start by looking at what you do and how you do it, especially the things you must do over and over again. Can you combine these repetitive tasks so you could be doing them together instead of separately? Figure out how much time, effort, money, and other resources it takes on average to line up a new customer. Set up parameters so that you're not beating a dead horse. Don't forget to stay in touch with your regular customers or they'll feel neglected and you risk losing them. Trust me on that one: I've made the mistake of taking good customers for granted and lost them as a result.

What about referrals, which are the best, strongest leads you have? For the past nine years, 95 percent of my business has been strictly referral. These people and companies are usually pre-sold by my other satisfied clients, prior to me even speaking with them. How easy is that? Don't forget a lot of concentrated work is put into any endeavor before referrals start coming your way, and still times arise when you must get off your backside and go out and hustle more work. Work *smarter not harder*, and *don't forget the only time "success" comes before "work" is in the dictionary.*

In my younger days I had the privilege of working in three fine-dining restaurants. At the first two, I was still in high school and worked as a busboy. In those restaurants, the busboy did practically everything for the customer. We set the table, broke down the table and brought the customers water, bread and every course that came out of the kitchen. We also took away the dishes for every course. We poured coffee, brought nonalcoholic beverages, pushed the dessert cart, etc. All the wait staff did was take the order, do the alcoholic drinks (I was a minor), set the food on the table (after I brought it out), and bring them their bill. My third restaurant job was as a fine-dining waiter. At that restaurant, we served and prepared the food tableside. I learned how to memorize their order without writing it down. I also learned how to become more efficient with my customers by always being a step ahead of their wants and needs. Now, when I see how the average waiter or waitress wastes their time with unnecessary movements it drives me crazy.

Let me give you an example in an average restaurant of what I'm talking about. The average waitperson wastes a good portion of their shift going back and forth to the kitchen for one item at a time instead of grabbing everything they need on every trip.

The act can be as simple as bringing out ketchup and mustard with a hamburger. Most of you have probably experienced this little scenario. You order a hamburger and fries; they bring it out and then ask you if you would like ketchup or mustard. Now while you're waiting, your food is getting cold and you're getting aggravated because you're thinking how inefficient the waitperson is for not asking you when you ordered your hamburger and fries if you wanted ketchup and mustard in the first place. Couldn't they just think ahead by anticipating the customers wants and needs. Most people use ketchup and mustard with their hamburger and fries, they should bring it out with the food or ask ahead of time. All they would have to do at that point would be to hand it to you, but instead they go running back to the kitchen, wasting time and money, not to mention ruining their tip.

How many times have you ordered a cup of coffee and after they bring it to you they ask, "Do want cream or sugar with your coffee?" Now your coffee's getting cold, so here we go again. Why not ask ahead of time or bring it with the coffee just in case?

Be smart, think before you act or move, and see if there's a better, faster, smarter way. Maybe no better way exists, but at least you'll be glad you thought about it first.

Life

Do you do anything in your life like an inefficient waitperson at a restaurant? I'm sure there's something. I'm not picking on you but rather I'm just asking you to think.

Story Twenty

When I was a youngster, my mom was a manicurist. She did it for about twenty-five years. Wherever she worked, the customers always said that she was the best manicurist they had ever had. Not only did she never cut anyone, but she put the polish on in one stoke. Ten fingers, ten strokes, and done. For those of you who have had a manicure, that's practically unheard of. Her clientele were some of the wealthiest and most influential people in Cleveland. If I mentioned some of the names regardless of where you live, you would know who they are.

I'm going to tell you what she taught me, which has made all the difference in my life:

> *"Always do your best, and always try to be better today than you were yesterday, regardless of what it is."*

Thanks, Mom!

Write down now: what experiences have you had when you figured out a way to do something smarter, not harder?

Write down now: what can you do or work on now on that you can do smarter, not harder, and that can make a difference in your business or your life? Whatever it is can be major or minor, preferably both.

CHAPTER TWELVE

WHEN IS A SALE SUCCESSFUL

WHEN

IS

A

SALE

SUCCESSFUL?

Oh, that's easy

WHEN *YOU*

MAKE MORE

THAN *YOU*

SPEND

DON'T TAKE

SOMETHING

SIMPLE

AND MAKE IT

COMPLICATED

Forget all those

Per-unit

Bean-counter ratios

They set you up for

Mindset Failure

YOUR OVERHEAD

OBLIGATIONS

CONTINUE

WHETHER YOU'RE

ADVERTISING/MAILING

OR NOT

That's why your overhead

DOESN'T BELONG

In the mix

After Your Sale

Take

THE GROSS PROFIT (from the sale)

Subtract

BOTH

The

Product cost

And your

ADVERTISING/MAILING

Costs

Whatever is left

Is

PROFIT

Period.

CHAPTER THIRTEEN

WHEN A SALE IS SUCCESSFUL

WHEN A SALE

IS

SUCCESSFUL...

1) DO IT AGAIN

2) DON'T MESS WITH IT

3) DO IT AGAIN

As the old saying goes...

IF IT AIN'T BROKE...

DON'T FIX IT

Advertising and Direct Mail

Have you ever been cooking something and while you're seasoning and tasting it you get the flavor just right? *Mmmm, that's good.* Then you go ahead and add one more ingredient to it and now you've ruined the taste. Now no matter how much you try and get back that great taste, you can't!

You can do exactly the same thing with a successful, proven sale or advertisement—whether it's direct mail, TV, radio, or print. I'm not saying that you shouldn't try and improve things, but some times you need to leave well enough alone, because it is working.

Ever try and tighten something too tight and you end up stripping it? You need to learn to feel when a connection is right; when it is right, all you have to do is massage it, not try and change it.

In direct mail, you run your mail piece until it stops doing what it was intended to do. At different times, the same mail piece will experience peaks and valleys. While you have one mail piece that's working, start on your next campaign and test it. With this approach, if your test mail piece doesn't work, you can go back and make changes and try again. During this time you still have your first one working. Once your have your second mail piece where it works, you're ready for round two when the first mail piece ceases to do its job. But don't stop there. Go to Round Three so you can always stay ahead of the game.

Story Twenty-one

A few years back when I was first starting out in the direct mail business I had a client who signed up for three sales of five thousand pieces each. I purchased a list of fifteen thousand names and did an A, B, and C split—we took an even amount from the same zip codes for each mail drop. This design tries to make each of the three lists as close to each other as possible and to ensure the most consistent response to the same mail piece.

On the first sale my client let me do what I know works and it did. We sold twenty cars in five hours. On the second sale, my client started making a few minor changes to the mail piece against my recommendation which was to leave it alone because it was working great. (*If it ain't broke, don't fix it.*) Those changes reduced the effectiveness of the second sale to twelve cars sold. Needless to say I was hot, and I pleaded with my client to do the third sale the same as the first. Not only did he not listen to me, but he insisted on changing it even more! (Remember what I said about adding one more ingredient to your recipe and ruining the taste? That's what he was doing. Instead of going back to the recipe of the one that tasted great, he kept adding ingredients.) The third sale was a dismal failure compared to the first; only seven cars were sold. Now here's the best part: he blamed me. Needless to say, I learned a great lesson and told the dealer we were done. What he did was the same as going into a restaurant's kitchen and adding ingredients to the chef's food, ruining the taste of the food, and then blaming the chef.

Remember: if what you're doing works great, leave it alone!

Sales

I can't tell you how many millions of sales have been ruined—or "bought back"—by the same salesperson that sold those goods or services in the first place. In these cases, the sale was made, but the salesperson did something to blow the sale so that it didn't take place (buying it back). Perhaps the sale "tasted" just right to the client, but then the salesperson added one more ingredient to a perfectly great-tasting product or service and wound up buying that product or service back.

The lesson here is to *learn when to shut up and quit selling.*

The scenario goes something like this. The client loves everything about what you're selling and then you tell them something that turns them off. Then they say "Oh, I didn't realize *that* (whatever you just said). Now I don't want it," and just like that it's over. Just like cooking, once you alter or ruin the taste you can't get it back. Another important lesson comes from the field of law: an attorney who is questioning a witness should never ask a question that the attorney doesn't already know the answer to.

In sales you don't tell a prospective client about a feature regarding your product or service before you find out whether or not that feature is important to them. How do you do that? By doing what I just did to you, simply by asking questions. Why, isn't that what you do?

A salesperson needs to learn, know, and feel when they've said enough and then to stop! Write up the sale, post-close, and then say good-bye, move on to the next one. And don't forget to check back with them to see if they're happy with what you sold them. Who knows? Maybe they'll order more or refer you to someone else.

Life

I'm confident that most of you have heard the expression "enough is enough." We see its manifestation in a lot of outward expressions such as wearing too much jewelry becomes gaudy, or wearing a wig or hairpiece that tried to become so real it looks fake. Perhaps someone is wearing so much cologne or perfume that they stink, or has applied so much makeup or grown so much facial hair that they've defeated the purpose of trying to look better. How about trying to dress so sexy that you wind up appearing slutty or trashy. Don't forget the men who try and act so macho or manly that they become Neanderthals. How about eating so much over so long a period of time that now you're sick, overweight, and in bad health.

"Enough is enough" also applies in relationships. Maybe we talk someone's ears off until they can't hear us anymore. Maybe we're being so controlling that the people we love rebel and even leave us. Giving too much love and affection that it becomes sickening is also possible. Love that's smothering does exactly that: it puts the love out.

The point that I'm trying to make with all these scenarios is that almost all instances of overcompensation really represent an undertone of insecurity, a feeling of not measuring up or fitting in. We sometimes think we're not good enough, but compared to who or what? Have you ever thought about that?

The greatest feeling of satisfaction is just being oneself. If people don't like or accept you for who and what you are, maybe you're trying to gain the affection of the wrong people.

You of course should be polite and respect other people's feelings and property, but if you have to act or try to be something or someone that deep down inside you're not, then maybe something is wrong with who you're trying to be. If you're not acting like yourself, something is wrong.

Always trying to make who and what you are better is great. That's totally different than what I've been saying about too much. Please don't get the two confused. They are actually opposites of the same thing. Try to improve on yourself, but do it in the right way. So what's the answer? Part of it is to *be who you are and love who you are, right where you are, and that will make you . . . the real star.*

Write down now about a time when you overcompensated for insecurities. Did you outgrow them yet? What did you learn from those experiences?

Write down now what your are overcompensating for, or using as a crutch that you're afraid to give it up. This question is hard I know. Do you really need to keep doing it if it makes you weaker not stronger?

CHAPTER FOURTEEN

PRICE, TIME, AND PERCEPTION

A

SUCCESSFUL

SALE

IS

ALL

ABOUT

PRICE

TIME

&

PERCEPTION

REMEMBER:

S.

P.

P.

P.

P.

SALE

PRICING

PERCEPTION

PRODUCES

PROFITS

Advertising

First, let's set a premise of what this chapter is really about. In order to do that we first need to define the two basic types of advertising. We'll call them type A and type B advertising.

Type A advertising is the kind that lets people know you exist. Type A sells service or low prices everyday or it can tell people about your product or service. Some examples are the Yellow Pages, billboards, business cards, sides of buses, buildings, trucks, your signs, advertising specialties, and many more. TV, radio, print, and direct mail can be used for either type A or B.

Type "B" advertising—the one we'll be addressing in this chapter—is what I call "short-term special sale advertising," for the few days or hours the regular prices are on sale. If you run a sale much longer than that, you'll defeat your purpose.

Type " B" ads have two main motivators: price and time. Combining these motivators yields a third: perception. The ideal is to have a perfect mixture of price and time. The mixture needs to create combustion just like in a car engine. *Combustion = Perception.* The proper amount of spark and fuel can make an engine run strong and fast. Most of us have experienced an untuned car that stalls, runs terrible, and because of that usually leaves you stranded in your driveway or at the side of the road. You need your mixture of price and time to run like a racecar. Otherwise your sale will leave you stranded in the bank line, scratching your head holding an empty deposit slip. You're probably saying to yourself; *how am I going to do all of that?* That's what this chapter is all about.

Price is the great motivator to action. Face it; everyone loves getting a deal and saving money. Keep in mind, however, that what you're selling must be something that people want or need. (No one is going to buy or want used toilet paper even if you're giving it away.) Want is much stronger than need.

We all know how it feels to have to buy something because you need it (like a new roof or new brakes on your car) as opposed to buying something (like a new outfit or a big-screen TV) simply because you want it. Most people land in debt by buying what they want instead of what they need. That's also what keeps the economy going, so let's use that premise to our advantage. *If you want to get rich you'll sell what other people want and buy only what you need, until you're rich.* (That sentence is a great pearl of wisdom I implore you to follow it if you want to be financially rich).

I'm confident that most of you have bought something you didn't want or need but the price was so good you bought it anyway. When you bought it you were thinking, *maybe I could use this some day.* I'll bet that item is still collecting dust, waiting to be used, and most probably, it never will be. Welcome to the great motivator: *price.*

Having a sale is usually all about saving money, especially to your potential customer or client. The sale needs to answer the question in the consumer's mind of "Why should I buy now instead of later, and why from you?" Sometimes terms— as in "no payments for six months" or "no down payment"— are as important or more compelling than price. If you can put price and terms together along with urgency, you're on your way to a successful sale.

When dealing with price, the main factor is the customer's perception of what makes a great deal or opportunity. If the customer doesn't think a compelling reason exists to buy now, your sale will flop. Remember that the fear of loss is greater than the desire for gain. If customers think they'll miss out on something they want or need, they are more apt to act on the offer NOW.

Knowing *how* to price a sale and *when* to have it is a real art. Every industry is different. When to have a sale and how often are the subjects of the next chapter.

Discounts are another factor when you're dealing with price and time. Let me put this point bluntly: Unless you're dealing in products that cost thousands of dollars, 10 percent off stinks! So does five hundred dollars off a new or used car. I'm sorry, it's just not enough. Remember that we're trying to motivate people to come into your store or to call you and use your services. The pull must be stronger! Nothing is wrong with those types of discounts or even more off once you're doing a transaction or if they see these types of discounts once they're in your store. But the discounts I previously mentioned are just not enough most of the time to cause a person to stand up from the couch, come in to where you are, and engage your services *right now*, and remember: having a successful sale is all about RIGHT NOW! Otherwise, why have a sale in the first place?

Price perception and discounts need to mean something to the consumer, not to you as the advertiser. Perception in this context means what the potential buyer thinks is happening or could happen. You need to give a substantial discount in order to compel action. Discounts like up to 30, 50 and even 70 percent off your regular prices are what I'm talking about. You don't have to give everything away but you do have to give away some profit in order to build more profits. Not everything needs to be discounted, but it helps. You probably missed the words "up to" a few sentences back—most people do—but those words save you from giving away too much, and they help you gain a lot. Even with the "up to" perception of the 30, 50, and even 70 percent off, the discounts are still there and still compelling to your customers.

Some of you are probably saying, "I can't discount my inventory that much or I'll go broke." First, this pricing is for a sale and it is not your everyday pricing. Second, if you don't have a substantial profit margin built into your product or service in the first place, statistics say you're going to go broke eventually anyway. So give it up (the specials or discounts), or don't have a sale and give it up. Bottom line: you need to make up your mind!

Not every discount needs to be in the form of "percent off." Lots of other ways are available to discount your product or service and still make money:

Buy one, get one free
Buy one at the regular price, get the second at half price
No payments for twelve months
Twelve months same as cash
No interest or payments for one full year
You're preapproved, or no one is turned down
(these credit specials are extremely important if
you're dealing with people who are credit challenged)
Bring in this certificate and save up to $3,275 on a new vehicle
(*that's one of mine*)
Free inspection
Buy two months of service, get the third month free.
Bring in a friend and save twice as much
(I just thought of that one)

The list goes on and on, and you should be grasping the idea. *The idea here is to come up with your own unique twist on this concept.*

Story Twenty-two

The other day I was talking to a friend of mine who just opened a furniture store. We were throwing around ideas and discounts on how to bring more business into his store.

His partner, who is very sharp and has been in the furniture business for quite a few years, told us about an instance when he went into a national recliner chair chain store that we'll call Lethargic Kid. The advertisement that brought him in said, "Two great chairs for one low price." He thought what most people think. It was buy-one-chair-get-the-second-chair-free. Guess what the offer really was? Buy two of their chairs at the regular price for each chair and they'll add the two chair prices together and give you the one "low price" for two chairs. How was that for misleading? The wording was so skewered that it fooled a real pro in the same business. As I said before, **I'm *not* saying** that you should mislead people, but you can really see how important perception really is.

Ever wonder what makes the consumer take advantage of a sale in the first place? W.I.I.F.M.—What's In It For Me? *People want to feel that they can buy something better, cheaper, or easier today over what they can buy tomorrow.* If you don't create that feeling, they won't be inclined to buy today, and *today's* sale is what it's all about. Again, why have a sale in the first place? Remember the chapter on urgency? Without urgency you have no energy, and no energy means no one is calling you or coming in to your store. Perception is everything, and urgency is a part of perception.

Story Twenty-three

I was in an office superstore buying White-Out. I don't remember the exact prices but it went something like this. One bottle of White-Out cost $1.29 and a three-bottle pack was $4.29. I called a clerk over and said, "This must be a mistake. If I buy a three-bottle pack, it will cost me more than if I buy three bottles separately. They must have the pricing switched; it always costs less to buy more." She checked the price and said, "No, that's the price." Now if I hadn't paid attention I would have spent more on a three-bottle pack than by buying one bottle at a time. How's that for store perception? We just assume quantity is cheaper, and the store was counting on that perception. At first I thought that pricing was a smart move on the part of the office superstore. But then again, maybe the move wasn't so smart because I left the store with the *perception* that the store was trying to get one over on me. I never forgot it. Don't mess with people, because you'll eventually and ultimately only wind up hurting yourself.

Write down now when you've been compelled by a sale and why. Give lots of examples.

Write down now: How can I use the above experiences and this new knowledge in having my own sales? Come up with some compelling reasons that someone should buy from you or your company as it relates to having a sale. Talk about your understanding as a well-informed consumer about other company's sales.

CHAPTER FIFTEEN

THE MARKET IS LIKE SOIL

The

Market

Is

Like

Soil

If you

PLANT and HARVEST

TOO OFTEN

The

MARKET

Will become

DEPLETED

Some would call that being Greedy

With no Patience

Remember the boy who
CRIED WOLF?

By crying WOLF
too many times
The consumer will

NO LONGER

take you

SERIOUSLY

and

Whatever

You do

From then on

Won't be

Perceived as

SPECIAL

If you

RARELY PLANT

You'll

RARELY HARVEST

That too will

DEPLETE

YOUR SOIL

It's called "Save a nickel, lose a dollar"

This also

ALLOWS

Your

COMPETITION

To

PLANT

And

HARVEST

<u>Your Customers</u>

and you'll

LOSE THEM

IF YOU WANT TO DO IT

RIGHT

DON'T HIT THE SAME PEOPLE

MORE THAN

4 TIMES

OR LESS THAN

2 TIMES

A YEAR

AND

MAKE IT

LOOK

DIFFERENT

EVERY

TIME

Advertising and Direct Mail

The last chapter talked about what makes a sale a sale. This chapter addresses how to keep your sale a sale and not ruin it. A sale needs to be something special, not something you have every day or even every month, at least not to or for the same people. You can run a private sale every week or even every month for that matter, just as long as the general public doesn't know about it and the target for every sale is different. Why am I saying this? A sale has to be an event or something really special to mean something to your prospective customer or client. Otherwise you're not running a sale; you're pulling a joke, and eventually that's how your customers or clients will perceive you . . . as a joke.

Think of a child who loves ice cream. We've all seen how excited children can become when they receive ice cream. Especially if they don't have it very often, ice cream is a real treat. Now let's take a child and give her ice cream every day. Not only that, let's give her as much ice cream as she wants at every serving. How long do you think it would take until the child was sick of ice cream? Not very long, I'm sure. How excited do you think the child would be now if you asked her, "Hey, do you want ice cream?" Do you really think that child now feels ice cream is a special treat? I doubt it. As a matter of fact she may now even hate ice cream, maybe for the rest of her life. In the same way, most retailers are over saturating us every day by continuously touting that "We're having a sale."

Let's look at the automobile business. A product and industry that is very near and dear to my heart. Unfortunately, the manufacturers in my opinion are making some huge mistakes right now. First, the manufacturers for the most part do not have their pulse on the dealer and or the consumer.

Take the Chrysler Corporation as an example. According to what I read in *USA Today*, in one of their quarters of 2001 they lost hundreds of millions of dollars by giving away too many and too much in customer rebates. How does something like that happen? Easy, by giving away too much, to too many too often. *Chrysler depleted their soil.*

Chrysler used to give away rebates of about one thousand dollars. After doing that for too long, the consumer yawned so Chrysler began giving away fifteen hundred dollars. Then came two thousand, twenty-five hundred, thirty-five hundred, and now even forty-five hundred dollars, maybe even with zero interest on top of that. Nothing is wrong with discounts, rebates, and low interest rates. I think they're great. What's wrong is that they've done it too often and for too long each time. By now when you see these special offers on TV, you say to yourself, "Yeah, so what? Give me something that will really motivate me to buy now." What Chrysler and a lot of the other auto manufacturers have done is now hard to fix. We as a society have become numb to their ads, so as a result *their specials aren't special anymore.*

How about regular retail? A chain that I'll call "Mattress Showers and Beyond" is a great store. My wife and I buy a lot of things for our house there. Every three weeks to a month we get a big postcard from them announcing that they're having a one item 20 PERCENT OFF SALE. We chuckle every time we receive one of their mailers, and we put it in a file for when we go there to shop. We use those coupons because they honor them expired or not. What they are offering isn't a real sale. If it were a real sale, the response would be terrible because nothing that happens so routinely every month is going to be perceived as very special.

One of the worst and most obnoxious sales is the going-out-of-business sale when the company is not really going out of business. Do you really want to deal with a company that blatantly lies to you? In order for a business to do well, the consumer must trust the business. You build people's trust by being honest with them, even if sometimes the information you give is to your detriment. On many occasions I have had to tell my clients something they didn't like or want to hear. It's even cost me money. The upside is that if you ask any of my clients if I'm honest and or if I can be trusted, I'm confident you would get a resounding "Yes." To me, that type of recognition is worth everything.

Story Twenty-four

Just yesterday my son Thomas helped me sum up the basis of this chapter in one word: *Credibility*. We were watching Super Bowl XXXVI and a commercial came on for another TV show. This network always advertises this show as "the episode you don't want to miss," which could be true. Thomas said to me, "They always advertise that show like that. Doesn't that ruin their credibility?" I thought for a second and said, "Yes, it does." A legitimate sale is all about credibility, which is all about believability. If the consumers don't believe you, they won't trust you or come to your sale. By crying wolf too often, you can deplete your soil and lose all credibility. *No credibility = No profitability.*

Now that we've spent time on what happens by doing too much too often, let's address not doing enough, often enough. Go back about 150 years and pretend that you live on a farm in a little town that is home to one of twenty farms. In the center of this little community is a twenty-acre parcel of fertile soil where you can grow your fruit and vegetables. Each of the twenty farms has one acre to do with as they please. What do you think would happen to your acre of land if you didn't spend enough time planting and tending to your soil? You probably wouldn't have much of a crop, which translated would mean that your family would not eat very well. Worse yet, weeds would overrun your parcel from neglect. If you neglected your soil long enough, little by little your neighbors' parcels would creep onto yours until your parcel ceased to exist, thereby starving out you and your family.

What does this little story have to do with advertising, direct mail, sales, relationships and life?

Everything! In advertising, direct mail, sales, relationships and life, if you don't stay in front of and in contact with your current and potential future customers or your significant other, you'll lose them to your competitors by default and neglect. For sales I don't mean you should be a pest. Just use the same common sense that I just covered earlier in this chapter. It's that simple.

Life

What do you do too much of in your life? Do you talk too much? Eat too much? Drink too much? Are you too needy, clingy, or greedy? Do you suffocate people with your actions and beliefs? Are you a real slob or a neat freak? Some of your extremes may drive other people crazy and chase them away. Do you expect too much from other people? Are you obsessive-compulsive? How about an addict? Any addiction is a "too much". Most of us are addicted to something or someone. We just can't get enough of _____ (fill in the blank: drugs, smoking, food, alcohol, caffeine, money, and even work—but there are many more addictions that are not as obvious, like play, shopping, golf, sports, clothes, shoes, TV, excitement, danger, jewelry, relationships, gambling, wanting or avoiding change, and that's just to name a few). Few people, places, or things are bad by themselves in moderation. Addiction arises when you can't be without something or other parts of your life are hurt by your obsession with that something.

How about being addicted to certain negative emotions, like anger, jealousy, fear, worry, selfishness, criticism, greed, envy, prejudice, and hate? Those emotions not only ruin your life, but they can also seriously damage and destroy your health.

What about not doing or being enough based on what you could *do or be.* Are you the type of person that always chooses the easy way out? Are you what I call an *At Leaster*™? At Leasters do the least amount possible, the bare minimum, just enough to squeeze by. They are always expecting things from other people. "It's not my job" is one of their most recognizable slogans. They think the world owes them a living and everything else for that matter. They always wait for someone else to do a particular task, or if they have to do something they do a lousy job because they figure you'll take the job away from them and do it right, thereby relieving them of their responsibility. They are the mooches of the world. They just don't want to be responsible for their own lives. They may be old in body but they have an " I don't want to grow up" attitude that pervades their total being.

"At Leasters" have what I call "*a couch potato mentality with a microwave mindset.*" They want everything now, but they don't want to work for it. This type of attitude is one of the biggest problems that we face in our society today.

The "At Leaster" plague especially infests our young people in school. Many children and young adults have great intelligence and receive lousy grades just because they're lazy. They don't know what it means to have to work for something.

They want everything now without having to work for it, and if they can't achieve what they want with little or no work, they quit. Part of this problem is not their fault. They've grown up in an instant gratification society. *Their brains are fertile, but they let the weeds of laziness take over their minds and bodies.*

If in the last part of this chapter I've hurt someone's feelings by what I have expressed, then I must have hit a nerve. If I have hit a nerve and upset you, then *grow up and take responsibility for your life!*

Truthfully I doubt that an "At Leaster" would even be reading this book. As far as I'm concerned, "At Leasters" are losers, and I seriously doubt that you're one of them. But if you are, there's still hope for you. It's all about your attitude and learning to work smart and hard for what you want.

What experiences has this chapter reminded you of? Write them down right here, right now before you go on to the next chapter.

Write down now: How can I use my experiences coupled with this new knowledge to improve on my business, relationships or life right now?

Oh . . .

by the way,

I don't suppose

You're
Interested

In making any more
$$$$$$$$$$$?

WE'VE HAD
LOTS OF CLIENTS
THAT SAID NO . . .
TO THAT QUESTION

FUNNY THING THOUGH

AFTER THAT. . .

WE MADE THEM

MILLIONS
$$$$$$$$$

Interesting, isn't it?

Remember that roller coaster

I told you about?

We're about to go

DOWN

One of those

Huge hills

Hang on

CHAPTER SIXTEEN

VICTOR or VICTIM

VICTOR?

OR

VICTIM?

EVERY DAY

IN

EVERY WAY

<u>YOU</u> CAN'T

ESCAPE IT

BUT <u>YOU</u>

DO

HAVE A

CHOICE

When I say "Victor or Victim, every day in every way™," I mean it. You have a choice of how you'll feel or react to every situation. I'm in no way saying that it's easy to think or react in terms of victor or victim. On the contrary, this type of thinking is difficult at times, but the rewards for doing so are incredible. Do you know what this really means? Do you understand and comprehend the magnitude of these statements? *You have it within your power to choose how you feel about everyone and everything in your life, and how you feel is your reality*. I know this statement is heavy, but stay with me.

The toughest part of this idea is: how do you choose to be a victor when you feel like a victim? Part of the answer is that you have to look at the world as one great classroom. All the students in your classroom are really your teachers with an ongoing lesson in mind, just for you.

Instead of saying or thinking that a thought, thing, word, person, or act is good or bad, hot or cold, right or wrong, you need to look at the big picture. Ask what is this thought, thing, word, person, or act trying to teach me. What is the lesson here?

The minute you stop reacting and start to analyze the situation as an outside observer, you the victim become the victor. If you want this approach to your life to really work, you need to be looking for the lesson you are supposed to learn, rather than view everything that happens to you through the victim's lens of *why me, why me?*
You choose your destiny, you make your choices, you choose how to react, you choose, you choose, you choose! That's some strong medicine and you probably don't want to believe it. Why? Because if you do believe what I'm saying here, you now realize that *all of your excuses from now on are gone!*

But it's true; if you choose to believe that all these choices are yours, you also must acknowledge that by believing these concepts, you are recognizing that *you and you alone are responsible for your life,* especially for the most part after the age of sixteen. The good news is that you can also take full responsibility for your accomplishments.

Taking full responsibility doesn't mean that you can do everything by yourself without any help from anybody ever again. No one is an island unto themselves. You must now however, with this knowledge, always do your best in everything you do—*not for what you gain, but for what you become in the process.* Because the more you become, the more you are.

Choosing to be the victor is a never-ending battle of vigilance and pain. The pain is in fighting for what's right, especially for what's right for you. But the alternative is feeling like garbage. As the victim, your self-image is poisoned right down to your core.

The good news is that the pain leaves you as each battle is won. Even through the pain, you still can feel good about yourself because of your convictions, such as the conviction of knowing that what you're doing is right for the betterment of a situation, someone else, or you.

The bad news is that the poisonous venom of being a victim can stay with you for ages and maybe forever. Sometimes to rid yourself of this venom, hard work is needed. You may have to endure short-term pain for long-term gain. You have to work at life for anything worthwhile you want. *Quality of life does not come easy.*

Maybe you're wondering why I describe these feelings so graphically? I speak and write from life experience, not conjecture or theory. Everything in this book is about life experience. If I've written this book correctly, most of the experiences that you read about here will ring true in your heart and mind because I triggered something in you from your own unique experiences. *Nothing is stronger to you than your own unique experiences.*

The choice of being the victor or the victim starts every day the moment you open your eyes in the morning. How do you feel, or more precisely, how do you choose to feel? Let's run through a little scenario of the choices we make to be the victor or the victim, every day in every way.

Do you wake up and you say to yourself "I feel great" (*victor*), or do you wake up and say to yourself "I feel lousy" (*victim*)? You get up, shower, and make breakfast, but you burn the toast. Do you get mad and start swearing at the toaster (*victim*), or do you say to yourself, "Boy, that looks interesting the way the toaster makes my toast all black and burnt," then you scrape off the burnt part, say it's no big deal and eat it anyway (*victor*)? Or do you say to yourself, "I think I'll choose to make another piece, turn the setting down, and watch it this time so it doesn't burn (*victor*).

Now you leave the house for work and within two minutes you are cut off in traffic by an inconsiderate driver. Do you start to cuss and scream at the driver and wish you had a cannon mounted on your hood so you could blow this inconsiderate S.O.B. to kingdom come? Not only that, do you get all aggravated in the process and your mind keeps thinking about what just happened for the rest of your drive to work (*victim*)? Then when you arrive at work you're still upset and someone says to you "Good morning" and you say to yourself "Yeah, what's so good about it" (*victim*)? Or when the inconsiderate driver cuts you off do you blow your horn and say to yourself, "Boy, they must be in a real hurry," and go back to enjoying your drive to work (*victor*)? When you arrive at work and someone says to you, "Good morning," you say out loud and think, "It sure is" (*victor*).

This little scenario is not unrealistic. Think of how many choices you and I need to make every day in just the first few hours. What about the rest of your day? *You must be ever vigilant or you'll become a victim before you know it, especially by default.*

Story Twenty-five

An interesting thing happened to me as I was writing this chapter that I think will drive home this last point. I was sitting at my desk writing. It was lunchtime, and I was getting really hungry and a little burnt out from being in front of the computer working for over three hours. My wife walked in and I said to her, "I'm HUNGRY. I have to go take a shower and go to the club and eat (*Victim*). Then she said, "Oh, Mr. Gets-up-when-he-wants, works-when-he-wants, does-what-he-wants has to take a shower, get into his new Jaguar and go to the country club for lunch. Boy, do you have it rough!" Then we both started to laugh. I've worked hard for everything I have. I'm living out my dreams and here I am half complaining about it. She really woke me up, in a good way. What I should have said is, "Boy, I'm hungry. I'm going to take a shower and then I get to go to the club for lunch" (victor), not "I have to." I almost made myself a victim by default, but my wife woke me up to what I was saying. Thanks, Honey!

How do you recognize if someone, including yourself, is in the mode of *victim* or *victor*? Usually their choice is written all over them (or you). Here are some telltale signs:

Mentally

Victim: negative, upset, aggravated, depressed, angry, moody, bored, not happy
Victor: positive, happy, joyful, calm, compassionate and loving

Verbally

Ask a person how they're doing today and their mindset comes pouring out:
Victim says, "not bad," "not too bad," "hanging in there"
Victor says, "good," "great," "terrific," "outstanding"

Approach to tasks

Victim: "I have to (do something)."
Victor: "I am going to [or I get to] (do something).:

Story Twenty-six

I was at one of my favorite car dealers. We had just finished a very successful sale and a few of us were sitting around talking. Our little group consisted of some managers and some top salespeople. Everyone in the group was making a good six-figure income. The date was around April 15, tax time, and we were complaining about how much we all had to give the government. The general manager, Joe, said that when he went to his accountant and the accountant said, "It's too bad you have to pay all this money in taxes," Joe said to him, "I'm happy I get to pay that much!" The accountant was floored and said, "What do you mean you're happy about having to pay this much in income tax?" Joe said, "You don't get it. I get to pay that much. Look at how much I was able to keep, and I wouldn't have been able to do that if I hadn't made all that money!"

We were all floored, too. We all looked at him and started saying "You get to pay."

He said with a big smile, "Yes, I get to pay, and it feels great!"

It took a few minutes for what Joe had said to sink in. After it did, I began saying, "Yeah, I get to pay," too. An interesting thing happens to your mindset when you say "I get to" instead of "I have to." By saying and thinking "I get to," your mindset becomes positive, whereby saying "I have to," the mindset stays negative. From that moment on, I get to pay my taxes!

More ways to distinguish victims and victors:

Physiology

Victim: Walks with no real purpose. They usually have their head down, shoulders hunched with no real stride to their step. They look like the world has beaten them. They sometimes rock from side to side as they walk, like they don't really know where they're going. When you were a kid, that type of walk was what your teacher probably called dilly-dallying.

Victor: The walk has purpose and a definite stride. Their head is held up and the shoulders are back. The look on the face and the bounce in the step indicates that the victor is going somewhere and has a definite purpose in mind.

Activities

Victim: An "At Leaster" does the least amount possible, or just enough to get by. Shows up late to work, or just in time, and leaves early or at the exact minute they're allowed to. Their famous retort is "I'm not paid to do that," or "It's not my job."

Victor: Always does more than is asked, a *Do Bester*™. Always doing their best in whatever they do. Shows up early to work, stays late, and they don't care whose job it is, just as long as it gets done. These are the self-starters and entrepreneurs of this world. The winners in life because they've worked hard and smart and they deserve it! Napoleon Hill always pounded away at *"going the extra mile" and "always giving more than is expected or paid for"*. That describes the victor.

In order to be a victor instead of a victim, you're going to need certain attributes.

Positive Attitude: You need to look for the good in life, and sure enough you'll find it. See the glass half full not half empty.

Friends and Family: No one is an island unto themselves. Everyone needs a support system, and no one is better than the people who love you.

Dreams: You need to believe in something better for yourself. You have to have hope. If you don't have hope, you'll probably end up on alcohol or dope. Excessive alcohol and dope erases your hope. Hope is the idea that there is always something better out there waiting for you. Hope gives you the feeling that *yes, it's possible.*

Goals: Dreams must have a way to manifest or become reality. Dreams without goals are just idle wishes, and wishes without action usually don't come true. Goals are the way we obtain our dreams.

Goals need to be written down. They also need to be specific and in the future or present tense with a specific deadline for their attainment. You need to read them at least three times a day, preferably out loud. Your goals should be broken down into small, measurable, attainable steps so that they are not overwhelming. Then, as Anthony Robbins says, "take immediate, massive action on those steps." Your deadline is always open to change. When you first write a goal, you don't always know how long achieving that goal will take. You can only guess. Don't let the fact that you sometimes won't make your deadlines stop you from dreaming your dreams. Just reset your target date and keep going.

Not every goal you set will be obtained. Don't let that stop you from setting new ones. I have not met a lot of goals or deadlines that I've set, especially as it pertains to writing this book. I just set new goals and keep going. Because this is one of the last chapters, you can see I'm almost there. (I have never written a book before so all I could do was guess. I didn't let minor setbacks such as not finishing when I thought I would stop me from completing my goal and neither should you.)

Set short-term, easy goals at first to get the hang of it and to gain confidence in yourself that you can do it. Whenever possible visualize and daydream about your goals completed with as much emotion as you can muster, especially each time you read them.

Belief: Beliefs are very personal, and without them we are just walking shells. *The first kind of belief is a belief in you*—in your abilities to do things and become someone who's a worthwhile human being, someone you can be proud of. If you don't believe in you first, convincing other people to believe in you is really hard. Lots of times, however, other people see great things in us that we don't see or want to recognize in ourselves, and they can help us bring those things out in us,

if we're willing to put forth the effort.

The second type of belief is in a power higher than ourselves. That higher power that's really running the universe. People of the Jewish and Christian faiths call this power God. The

Moslems call it Allah; some call it the Tao or Chi. Outside of the religious sects, this higher power might be nature, energy, spirit, and universal consciousness. Hundreds of names have been used for this power over the last ten thousand years. You can call it whatever you want, but you'll never really understand it. No one will. "The finite mind can never comprehend the infinite". All you can do is believe in it.

Not sure this higher power really exists? What do you think is controlling the trillion-plus cells in your body that are doing what scientists estimate are ten thousand functions every second? What's controlling the digestion in your body right now? Surely it's not you. After you swallow your food, you have no say-so as to what is happening with it. Ever wonder where the power comes from to make your heart beat? What about how a baby forms from just two cells. These questions are yours to answer. Earlier I said that you are responsible for you and your actions, which may in the light of this discussion sound like a slight contradiction regarding free will. This philosophical question has been pondered for years. Suffice to say we're not going to answer it here. My point is that, regardless of what you want to call it, if you don't believe that something higher than yourself is running the world, you're in for a real world of hurt.

Regarding your circumstances in dealing with other people, you don't always have to be the victim. For instance, at the dry cleaners, did they do a good job (*victor*) or are the same stains still there with an added bonus of a broken button at no extra charge and you made no comment to them about it (*victim*)? Think about how many times a week we end up settling for inferior work or service, which is getting less than we paid for. Sometimes it's just easier to let it go, or perhaps you think the situation is not worth your time and energy to argue about it.

But when we take that approach, we're letting "At Leasters" stay "At Leasters" by not holding them accountable for their actions and attitudes. By letting them skate away with slack performance, we're also saying that it's okay not to do a job right and that we're not worthy of the quality we were expecting in the first place. In doing so, we place ourselves squarely in *victim* status. If you're surrendering too often for your own comfort and well being *you need to stand up for yourself and make them do it right! Be a Victor and not a Victim!*

One of worst places consumers get taken advantage is in restaurants. How many times have they messed up your order, and when you tell them, "This is not what I ordered," they look at you like it's your fault? More times than you can probably count. The question is do you usually let them get away with it (*victim*), or do you send it back and make them do it right (*victor*)? Anyone who has gone out to eat with me can tell you that without hesitation I send it back ninety-eight out of one hundred times and make them do it right, and I don't care if they like it or not. That's what I ordered, that's what they promised, that's what I'm paying for, and that's what I expect, period. If you can't do something right, you shouldn't say or advertise that you can. They should be honest and tell you, "We're not very competent here, you'll have to take what we give you. If you're expecting it done the way you ask for, you'll have to go somewhere else." Unfortunately that scenario never happens. They tell you that you can have what you ask for, but you rarely get it. So what's the alternative? The alternative is standing up for yourself because you'll feel better about yourself for doing so, you'll make them accountable, and you'll be glad you did (*victor*).

Story Twenty-seven:

I was in Atlanta on business and I was with my friends Jim and Rosemary Sullivan. We decided to go to Morton's Steak House. I told them how I really felt like a steak but I had a problem. The problem was that I like my steak with no pink on the inside. Doesn't sound like a big deal, does it? Ask anyone who likes their steak like me, and they'll tell you it almost never comes out well done enough, it's still pink.

My biggest challenge with that situation is that when my food doesn't come out the way I ordered it, I send it back. Now whomever I'm eating with eats their food while I watch. Just about the time they are finished, out comes my food, and now I eat while they watch. Sounds like a lot of fun, doesn't it? I don't know about you, but when I go out and eat with someone I'd really like to eat at the same time they do. Call me crazy, but isn't that what going out to eat with someone is supposed to be about? That was my impression of the concept.

So while were walking to Morton's I tell them what I just told you, and I said I really want to eat at the same time as you two do. So I thought for a minute and came up with a way to hold them accountable for getting my food order correct. Here's how it went.

Our waiter comes over. Jim and Rosemary both order a thick steak rare. I order steak medallions well done. (I'm really in trouble now, because anytime someone with me orders a steak on the red side getting mine with no pink inside is double hard.) When I ordered, I asked the waiter Leonard if he could promise to make sure my steak was well done. He said sure.

I said, "Could you guarantee it?"

He said, "What do you mean?"

I said, "I'll make an agreement with you. You get my steak the way I want it the first time out and I'll tip you big. On the other hand if it comes out with any pink on the inside you bought my dinner."

At first he didn't want to do it, but when I really challenged him to put his money where his mouth was, then he agreed. When he walked away, I told my friends, "I hope he gets it right, but if he doesn't he's buying my dinner."

Now keep in mind these steak medallions are only two to three inches in diameter and only half an inch thick. On a hot open flame, how long could it take to get these medallions so there's no pink on the inside, five minutes if not less? Guess what happened when they brought them out twenty-five minutes later? You guessed it: The medallions were rare, so rare in fact that I knew it even before I cut into them. (There's a method in a lot of restaurants that I think is a big mistake. That method is to have someone other than the person who took your order bring it out. How does the person know if what they're bringing you is exactly what you ordered? They don't, and that's one of the problems in this situation.) The minute that person brought out my food and I cut into it, I said, "Send it back and tell Leonard he just bought my dinner". The maitre d' came over and asked what was wrong, I told him and he apologized and said he would make it right. So there I was again, watching someone else eat. Luckily the medallions only took a few minutes to make right, and I was able to eat most of my meal with my friends.

A few minutes later Leonard came over steaming mad, not at us but at the chef. He told us that he explicitly told the chief three times how to cook my food and basically the chef ignored his instructions. He then apologized for the mistake and then told me my meal was free.

Here comes the good part and the reason that I would go back there. Leonard then said, "I have put in three Godiva Chocolate cakes for dessert, one for each of you. They'll take about twenty minutes, so while you're waiting, pick out three more desserts to eat now." We said, "No, that's okay, we'll wait." Leonard insisted that we take three desserts while we wait. We did, and they were great. Then out came the Godiva cakes, and they were incredible. We were not finished yet. After we finished the cakes, they brought over a complimentary dessert wine tray with aged ports and sherries. We indulged, and after that point we were—needless to say—happy and stuffed. Bottom line was this: my meal was free and we received over eighty dollars in complimentary treats to apologize for the mistake. How's that for turning what could have been a *victim* meal into a *victor* feast! Now don't misunderstand me. I always think you should pay for what you get, but sometimes it's really nice to be compensated for being inconvenienced.

Oh, by the way, are you wondering about Leonard's tip? It was big. Anyone that goes to all of that effort and expense to make a bad situation right deserves a big tip. (If you don't already tip at least 20 percent minimum for good service, you're being cheap and shame on you. If you do tip well, congratulations for doing what you know to be the right action.)

Here comes a really big and important question for you.

I would highly recommend pondering it intently:

IN YOUR LIFE
AND
IN YOUR BUSINESS
<u>DO</u> <u>YOU</u>

PLAY
NOT TO
LOSE
?

OR

DO YOU

PLAY

TO

WIN!!!

?

Playing not to lose stems from fear. On the other hand, playing to win comes from faith. *Victor* or *victim* is how you look at any given situation (things, thoughts, acts, etc.). Playing to win vs. playing not to lose is how you go after or deal with whatever it is that you want to do or be.

An example could be a football game. Think of the bend-don't-break prevent defense (playing not to lose) vs. the explosive West Coast offense (playing to win). Have you ever noticed in a football game how a team goes in at halftime winning by a huge margin then loses the game in the second half? What often happens in those situations is really quite simple. In the first half the team with the huge margin was playing to win. In the second half, they didn't want to lose their lead, so they started playing it safe (playing not to lose). In the meantime, the team that was down at the half has nothing to lose since their already losing, and they go for the win. The momentum has shifted, and the team that's playing to win, wins. You should always play to win. You'll be surprised quite often at the good that comes out of working and playing with that attitude.

An interesting indicator is available to you of how someone goes after life. This indicator is not an exact science, but for the most part it seems to have some significant relevance:

How people go into a swimming pool is a mirror of how they go into and after life. Some just dive right in and deal with the consequences (possible cold water); others feel it first and then dive in; many others still go in very carefully and cautiously one step at a time, trying to get used to the water. Some never put their head or face in, some only dangle their feet, and some won't even go in at all. The next time you go to a pool, watch how people go in the water with this idea in mind. You'll get a kick out of it, along with some insight into how people deal with life.

What experiences has this chapter reminded you of? Write them down right here, right now.

Write down experiences of when you felt like a victim and what you did to turn it around to be the victor.

Write down now: How can I use my experiences coupled with this new knowledge to improve on my business or life right now?

CONCLUSION

IT'S LOOK IN THE MIRROR TIME

Guess

What

Time

It is?

It's

LOOK

IN

The

MIRROR

TIME

<u>DO</u> <u>YOU</u>

SIT DOWN

And

WATCH

THINGS

HAPPEN?

Or . . .

<u>DO</u> <u>YOU</u>

STAND UP

And

MAKE

THINGS

HAPPEN?

Well . . .

WHA
It Go
B

T'S

ing to

E?

Now that you have all this information and knowledge, what are you going to do with it? You're probably expecting some rah-rah pep talk for the last chapter. Sorry, I'm going to nail you between the eyes with some hard-hitting truths. The book is over and there's no more coddling!

Chances are that even after reading this book you're not likely to change the way you go through life, unless you really, really want to. Why? Because the way you conduct yourself is too deeply ingrained in you, and you probably don't want to change bad enough.

So here's my advice: Know and be aware of where you're really coming from. *What is or are the catalysts of your feelings and opinions?* If you're like most people, the answer is one of two emotions, either faith or fear, and one of two motivators, gaining pleasure or avoiding pain. In other words are you running from, avoiding things, and procrastinating (sitting down and watching things happen)? Or are you doing everything that you know you should do and going towards what you want (standing up and making things happen)? *You need to figure out where your motivation or inclinations are coming from, based on the catalysts I just told you about. Then make your decisions intelligently with knowledge based on your goals and what you want out of life.* Always keep in mind that your decisions affect more than you realize and should be made with the idea of the overall good for you, your loved ones, and the universe. *You can't get much smarter than that.*

Here's another truth: You get out what you put in, and you get what you pay for, whether the forum is business, relationships, or life in general. The currency might be money, time, effort, energy, or support. Anything can be a contributing factor. Just remember: If you try and save a nickel on the wrong things or people, you'll lose a dollar by not giving everything your all.

Is it easy? Are you kidding? It's almost impossible! But what a worthy goal for you to aspire to:

Always doing your best in everything you do, not only because of what you will gain, but also because of what you will become in the process.

Just imagine how great and wonderful you will feel and things will be if you purposely live your life that way.

You

WHAT an

You

ABSOLU

Are

d WHERE

Are...

TELY!!!...

BEC

o

WH

You

AUSE

f

O

Are

NOTH

Ca

CHA

Un

YOU

ING

n

NGE

til

DO

POSTSCRIPT

Writing and finishing this book has been a twenty-year dream. *Realized.*

My sincere hope is that you have enjoyed and gained something wonderful from this book —whether that something wonderful is an idea, a confirmation of what you already knew, or a good laugh now and then during your reading. I suggest that you read this book again, if not right away then maybe at least once a year. You'll be amazed how much more you will learn and can use after trying and implementing some of the ideas and concepts herein, and then reading it again to realize that and getting even more out of it.

I think you'll also find that most of what I've expressed here you can use in some way, shape, or form. I would be delighted to hear from you as to how this book has affected or impacted your business, relationships and life. Serving you has been an honor and a pleasure, until next time. . . .

Sincerely,

David Alan
April 2003

SUGGESTED READING

Business

Positioning: The Battle for Your Mind, Al Ries and Jack Trout
Who Moved My Cheese, Spencer Johnson MD
Lip Service, Hal Becker
The End of Marketing As We Know It, Sergio Zyman
Can I Have 5 Minutes Of Your Time?, Hal Becker
How to Master the Art of Selling, Tom Hopkins
Secrets of Closing the Sale, Zig Zigler
Rich Dad Poor Dad, Robert T. Kiyosaki
The Greatest Secret in the World, Og Mandino
22 Immutable Laws of Branding, Al Ries and Laura Ries
You Can't Teach a Kid to Ride a Bike at a Seminar,
    David H. Sandler
How to Win Friends and Influence People, Dale Carnegie
Selling the Wheel, Jeff Lox and Howard Stevens
Under the Radar, Jonathan Bond and Richard Kirshenbaum
The Jewish Phenomenon, Steven Silbiger
The Little Money Bible, Stuart Wilde
Law of Success, Napoleon Hill
Guerrilla Publicity,
Jay Conrad Levinson, Rick Frishman and Jill Lublin
The 100 Absolutely Unbreakable Laws of Business Success,
    Brian Tracy
Instant Rapport, Michael Brooks
The 7 Habits of Highly Effective People, Stephen R. Covey
Direct Mail Workshop, Rene' Gnam
The Power to Get In, Michael A. Boylan

Life

Life is Tremendous, Charles 'Tremendous' Jones
Thoughts Are Things, Edward Walker
Power of Concentration, Theron Q. Dumont
Rays of the Dawn, Thurman Fleet
As a Man Thinketh, James Allen
Until Today, Iyanla Vanzant
Get With the Program, Bob Greene
Natural Healing with Herbs, Humbart "Smokey" Santillo
Food Enzymes "The Missing Link to Radiant Health.
   Humbart "Smokey" Santillo
Awaken the Giant Within, Anthony Robbins
Unlimited Power, Anthony Robbins
Live Your Dreams, Les Brown
Feng Shui Made Easy, William Spear
The Purpose of Your Life, Carol Adrienne
Clear Your Clutter with Feng Shui, Karen Kingston
Bhagavad Gita, Yogi Ramacharaka
What to Say when You Talk to Yourself, Shad Helmstetter PH.D.
Power of Now, Eckhart Tolle
Tuesdays with Morrie, Mitch Albom
Door to All Wonders, Tao Huang and Mantak Chia
T'ai Chi Classics, Waysun Liao
Mastering Chi, Hua'Ching Ni
Tao Te Ching, Lao Tzu Translated by Stephen Mitchell
The Seasons of Life, Jim Rohn C.P.A.E.
The Mystical Magical Marvelous World of Dreams,
   Wilda B. Tanner
The Man Who Tapped the Secrets of the Universe, Glenn Clark
The Precious Present, Spencer Johnson MD
Ki in Daily Life, Koichi Tohei
The Body Reveals, Ron Kurtz and Heckter Prestera,M.D

*Remember: Your business is only a part of your life. The better
your life is, the better your relationships and business will be.*

David Alan

David Alan is the quintessential entrepreneur. With over 30 years and 70 businesses and careers under his belt "experience" should be his middle name.

As the president and CEO of *MAIL-RITE INTERNATIONAL® INC.* David has helped his clients generate over 200 Million Dollars in revenue in just a few short years. His unorthodox, against the grain maverick style has made him a leader in the field of Direct Mail Advertising. Consistently on the cutting edge David is always pushing the envelope to try something new and fresh.

Not only has David helped train hundreds of salespeople, he has been fondly referred to as a pro's pro by some of the best sales trainers in the business.

David also holds a teacher's degree from the Concept Therapy Institute where through them and other sources he has spent thousands of hours studying and understanding the human condition.

An electrically charged enthusiastic speaker and trainer David helps to instill common sense tactics in real world situations. When a company or organization needs a fresh new approach David Alan is their first call.

SERVICES
AVAILABLE FROM
DAVID ALAN

- Advertising – Direct Mail
- Consulting – Advertising and Sales
- Lists – Postal Mail and E-mail
- Speaker – Key Note
- Seminars
- Workshops
- Order Additonal Copies of this Book

TO CONTACT DAVID ALAN,
CALL, WRITE OR E-MAIL:

MAIL-RITE INTERNATIONAL® *INC.*
PO Box 391375
Solon, Ohio 44139-8375
440-519-1515 or 866-519-1515
www.Mail-rite.com
E-mail: Da@Mail-rite.com

www.100Milliondollar.com

NOTES